Wi-Fi Home Networking
Just the Steps™

FOR

DUMMIES®

by Keith Underdahl

WILEY

Wiley Publishing, Inc.

Wi-Fi Home Networking Just the Steps™ For Dummies®

Published by
Wiley Publishing, Inc.
111 River Street
Hoboken, NJ 07030-5774
www.wiley.com

Copyright © 2006 by Wiley Publishing, Inc., Indianapolis, Indiana

Published by Wiley Publishing, Inc., Indianapolis, Indiana

Published simultaneously in Canada

For general information on our other products and services, please contact our Customer Care Department within the U.S. at 800-762-2974, out- side the U.S. at 317-572-3993, or fax 317-572-4002.

For technical support, please visit www.wiley.com/techsupport.

Wiley also publishes its books in a variety of electronic formats. Some content that appears in print may not be available in electronic books.

Library of Congress Control Number: 2005939193

ISBN-13: 978-0-471-78328-2

ISBN-10: 0-471-78328-5

Manufactured in the United States of America

10 9 8 7 6 5 4 3 2 1

1B/TQ/QT/QW/IN

WILEY

About the Author

Keith Underdahl is an electronic publishing specialist, network administrator, and freelance writer from Oregon. He has written numerous books, including *50 Fast Windows XP Techniques*, *Digital Video For Dummies*, 4th Edition, *Adobe Premiere Elements For Dummies*, and more.

Author's Acknowledgments

First and foremost I wish to thank my family for putting up with me through another book project. I pray that I am not irradiating them with all of this Wi-Fi gear.

I want to thank Wiley for bringing me on for this exciting new book, and to the Wiley publishing team who helped put it all together. Beth Taylor's outstanding editing helped turn my work into something intelligible, and Dan DiNicolo provided valuable feedback as technical editor.

I also had help from various industry people, including David Blumenfeld, David King, Andy Marken, Jacqueline Romulo, and Marleen Winer. Thanks folks!

Publisher's Acknowledgments

We're proud of this book; please send us your comments through our online registration form located at `www.dummies.com/register/`. Some of the people who helped bring this book to market include the following:

Acquisitions, Editorial, and Media Development

Project Editor: Beth Taylor

Acquisitions Editor: Melody Layne

Copy Editor: Beth Taylor

Technical Editor: Dan DiNicolo

Editorial Manager: Jodi Jensen

Media Development Coordinator: Laura Atkinson

Media Project Supervisor: Laura Moss

Media Development Manager: Laura VanWinkle

Editorial Assistant: Amanda Foxworth

Cartoons: Rich Tennant (`www.the5thwave.com`)

Composition Services

Project Coordinator: Erin Smith

Layout and Graphics: Denny Hager, Heather Ryan, Brent Savage, Erin Zeltner

Proofreaders: Cindy Ballew, Leeann Harney

Indexer: Sherry Massey

Publishing and Editorial for Technology Dummies

Richard Swadley, Vice President and Executive Group Publisher

Andy Cummings, Vice President and Publisher

Mary Bednarek, Executive Acquisitions Director

Mary C. Corder, Editorial Director

Publishing for Consumer Dummies

Diane Graves Steele, Vice President and Publisher

Joyce Pepple, Acquisitions Director

Composition Services

Gerry Fahey, Vice President of Production Services

Debbie Stailey, Director of Composition Services

Contents at a Glance

*I*f you have more than one computer, a home network can be pretty handy. With a home network you can share files, printers, and Internet connections. Your home network may also connect devices such as game consoles, PDAs, digital media players, security cameras, and more. And thanks to modern wireless networking technologies, it's now easier than ever to create a large, useful home network without turning your home into a rat's nest of cables.

About This Book

Networking is an advanced computer topic, which means that many networking books are dry and difficult to follow. But some people just want to get their network up and running, and they're not terribly interested in reading a lot of discussion of network theory and concepts. If this sounds like you, then I hope that this is your book. Following the *Just the Steps* style, this book includes only the essential steps you need to perform common home networking tasks.

Why You Need This Book

Networks are a lot more fun to use than to configure. If you want to start using your wireless network right away, this book can help you get things functioning quickly. Each task covers a specific subject, and most steps take only a minute or two to follow. Think of this as the anti-computer computer book, because it's all about less reading and more networking.

Introduction

Conventions used in this book

➡ When you have to access a menu command, I use the ⇨ symbol. For example, if you have to open the File menu and then choose Open, I say File ⇨ Open.

➡ Internet addresses are presented like www.dummies.com. I leave off the http:// part of Web addresses because you usually don't have to type it anyway.

 When you see this icon, the text includes helpful tips or extra information relating to the task.

How This Book Is Organized

I organized the chapters of this book into several basic parts:

Part 1: Starting a Wireless Network

This part shows you how to get your home network started. I show you how to set up a wireless access point, connect wireless computers — both Windows PCs and Macs — to the access point, and share your Internet connection with the network.

Part 11: Securing Your Network

If you aren't careful, intruders can easily access your wireless network, stealing your Internet access and accessing your personal files. This part helps you secure your home network from intrusion.

Part 111: Improving Your Network's Performance

Does your network seem a little slow? Does the connection drop out frequently? This part helps you improve the performance of your network, as well as identify and fix network problems.

Part 1V: Using Someone Else's Network

Wireless networks are popping up everywhere, and if you have a Wi-Fi-equipped laptop or PDA you may be able to use hotspots and other public wireless networks. The chapters in Part IV show you how to use hotspots, connect two computers directly to each other wirelessly, and network your computer with Bluetooth devices, such as headsets and GPS receivers.

Part V: Practical Applications

These chapters help you perform some common networking tasks, such as networking game consoles, playing digital music and videos from anywhere in your home, using Internet telephony, and more.

Get Ready To

If you're setting up your first home network, or if you're trying to use a public hotspot, there's a task in this book to get you started right away. So jump right in and get connected!

Part I
Starting a Wireless Network

The 5th Wave   By Rich Tennant

WIRED HOME OF THE FUTURE

"I'm setting preferences – do you want Turkish or Persian carpets in the living room?"

Setting Up Wireless Access Points

If you want to do wireless networking, your first step is to install a wireless access point. All of your wireless gear — laptops, PDAs, cameras, media centers, printers — connects to your network using radio waves instead of cables, and a *wireless access point* (WAP) is the device that creates your radio wave network.

As the name implies, a wireless access point gives wireless devices access to a network. The network may include other devices that are connected by Ethernet cables, or the network may consist entirely of wireless connections. Whatever type of network you need, your first step in setting up a wireless network is to buy and configure a WAP. In this chapter, you discover how to:

⟶ **Select a wireless access point:** The market now offers many different wireless access points from which to choose. I go over how to select a model that meets your needs and budget.

⟶ **Set up the hardware:** After you purchase a WAP, you need to set it up and make all the necessary hardware connections to make it work.

⟶ **Take the first steps towards creating a secure network:** Wireless networks are extremely handy, but if left unsecured, they also leave your personal files open to theft and your Internet connection available to strangers.

⟶ **Manage your network remotely:** You can control your wireless network even if you're on the other side of the country.

Chapter 1

Get ready to . . .

Choose a Wireless Access Point

1. Decide if the wireless access point (WAP) will also serve as a router.

    A router allows your network to share a broadband (cable or DSL) Internet connection, as well as connect your wireless devices to Ethernet wired computers. WAPs with built-in routers are widely available.

2. Count the number of Ethernet cable ports on the WAP.

3. Use a router/WAP with four Ethernet ports (see Figure 1-1) or a router/WAP/DSL modem with only one Ethernet port (see Figure 1-2).

    At the very least, a WAP/router should have an Ethernet port labeled *WAN* for connecting to a broadband modem. WAN stands for *wide area network* and usually refers to a very large network such as the Internet. You may also need some *LAN* Ethernet ports for connecting to Ethernet wired computers. Your home network is a LAN, which stands for *local area network*.

4. Determine which Wi-Fi standards your WAP needs to support.

    The 802.11g standard is faster than 802.11b, and 802.11g WAPs are backwards-compatible with 802.11b devices. If you also have 802.11a gear, you'll need a WAP that supports 802.11a.

Figure 1-1: Access point with four Ethernet ports.

Figure 1-2: Access point with one Ethernet port.

Configure Your Wireless Hardware

1. Connect your WAP to a computer using an Ethernet cable.

    If your ultimate plan is to connect all devices wirelessly, you can disconnect this Ethernet cable later, after you have finished configuring your WAP and router.

2. If you have a broadband modem, connect it to the WAN port on your wireless access point using an Ethernet cable.

3. Make sure that the modem is on and connected to your Internet Service Provider (ISP). Your hardware should be set up similar to the configuration shown in Figure 1-3.

4. Start up your computer.

    If your computer has Windows 2000, Windows XP, or Mac OS X, make sure that you log in with a user account that has administrator rights.

5. Plug in the power connector for the WAP and, if the WAP has a power switch, turn it on at this time.

6. After you have logged in to the router and performed the initial setup (as I describe later in this chapter), you can disconnect the Ethernet cable and link all of your computers wirelessly, as shown in Figure 1-4.

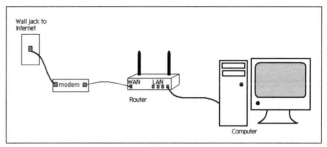

Figure 1-3: Temporarily connect the WAP to a computer.

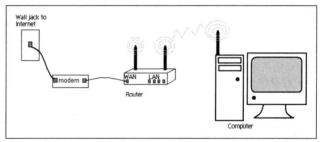

Figure 1-4: Disconnect the Ethernet cables and network wirelessly.

 For best performance and Wi-Fi range, position your wireless access point as high as possible and away from metal or stone walls. Also avoid placing the WAP near electronic devices, such as microwave ovens and the base units for 2.4 GHz cordless phones.

Log In to the Access Point

1. Launch a Web browser, such as Internet Explorer, and click Stop in the browser toolbar to stop any Web pages from loading.

2. In the Address bar, type the default IP address for your access point and press the Enter key. If the connection is successful, you should see a log in dialog box (see Figure 1-5).

3. Enter the default administrative user name and password for your WAP. (The default password should be listed in the WAP's documentation. Often, the default user name is blank and the default password is admin.)

Change the Admin Password

1. Log in to the router WAP using a Web browser (refer to the previous task).

2. Click the tab that contains administrative controls. (On some routers, admin controls are located on the Tools tab, as shown in Figure 1-6.)

3. Type your new password in both of the password text boxes provided.

 Try to choose a password that is somewhat complex; include both letters and numbers. Avoid easily guessed passwords, such as the name of your pet, and keep in mind that passwords are usually case-sensitive. The router's password should be changed as soon as possible because hackers know the default passwords programmed into new routers.

4. Click OK or Apply.

Figure 1-5: Use the default admin name and password.

 192.168.0.1 is the default IP address for many WAP/routers. Linksys routers usually use the IP address 192.168.1.1 instead. If Internet Explorer is unable to connect to this address, check the router's documentation to see if you should use a different IP address.

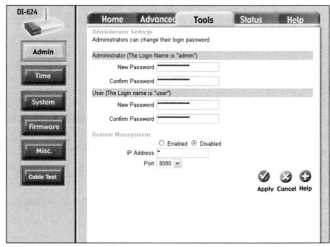

Figure 1-6: Administrative controls.

Set the SSID

1. Log in to the access point and find the wireless controls. Most access points have a Wireless tab or a Wireless button (see Figure 1-7).

2. Enter a word in the SSID text box.

 SSID is the name that wireless devices use to identify your access point. If you want to keep your wireless network more private from others, choose a cryptic SSID like the one shown in Figure 1-8, which combines letters and numbers.

3. Click OK or Apply.

Activate the Wireless Radio

1. Log in to the access point and find the wireless controls. Most access points have a Wireless tab or a Wireless button.

2. Select the On radio button, as shown in Figure 1-8, and click OK or Apply.

 If you are going to be away for several days, temporarily turn off the wireless radio to prevent others from using your wireless signal.

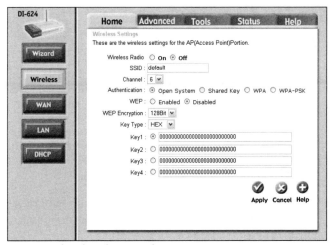

Figure 1-7: The radio and SSID controls.

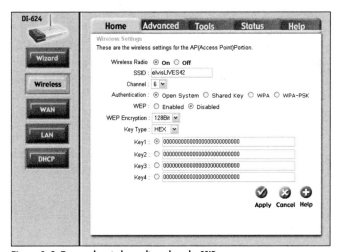

Figure 1-8: Turn on the wireless radio and set the SSID.

Set Up Remote Access Point Management

1. Determine the IP address for the computer from which you want to be able to access your router/WAP over the Internet.

    To quickly determine the IP address of the computer on which you are currently working, visit a Web site such as www.what ismyip.com or www.showmyip.com. Your computer's current IP address appears on-screen.

2. At your local network, log in to the router/WAP control panel and open the controls for remote access management (see Figure 1-9).

3. In the IP Address text box, enter the IP address of the computer that will be remotely managing your router, as shown in Figure 1-10.

    If the remote computer has a dynamic IP, or if you don't know what computer you'll be using for remote management, just enter an asterisk (*) in the IP Address box, as shown in Figure 1-9. Doing this allows any computer at any IP address to access the router, provided it has the correct password.

4. Specify the port that will be used to access the router. If you are accessing the router over the Internet using a Web browser, choose Port 80, which is the port used by Web browsers.

5. Enable remote management and click OK or Apply to apply your settings.

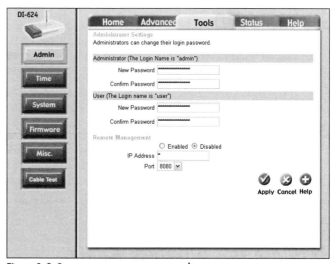

Figure 1-9: Remote access management controls.

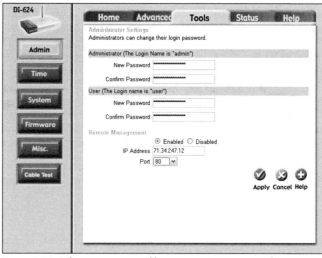

Figure 1-10: Only a computer at IP address 71.34.247.12 can access this router.

Manage Your Access Point Remotely

1. Launch a Web browser on the remote computer.

2. In the Address bar of the Web browser, enter the IP address for your home network, followed by a colon, and then the port number specified in your router for remote access (see Figure 1-11).

 Remember, you need to determine your home IP address while you are actually at home, using your home network. I go over how to do this in the previous task.

3. Press the Enter key.

4. Log in to your router/WAP using your administrative account name and password, as shown in Figure 1-12.

 After you are logged in you should be able to perform all administrative tasks of your router/WAP as normal.

I strongly recommend that you disable remote management when you are not using it. When remote management is enabled, hackers can more easily gain access to your router's control panel over the Internet and gain access to the rest of your network.

Figure 1-11: Enter the IP address and port for your home router/WAP.

Figure 1-12: Log in to your router/WAP.

Configuring Your Network

*B*efore your wireless devices can talk to each other, you are going to have to do some basic network configuration. Setting up networks is pretty easy these days, especially if you use the Windows Network Setup Wizard to walk through the setup process. But some things may need to be configured manually. In this chapter, I go over how to configure those items and change them later if necessary. You find out how to:

➡ **Set a network's workgroup name:** You can think of the workgroup name as the name of your network. The workgroup name needs to be the same on all of your computers in order for them to see and communicate easily with each other.

➡ **Set up DHCP:** Each computer on your network is identified by a unique IP address. A Dynamic Host Configuration Protocol (DHCP) server is the program that hands out IP addresses to each computer on the network.

➡ **Use Windows Internet Connection Sharing (ICS):** If you have one computer that connects directly to the Internet through a modem, you can share that computer's Internet connection using Windows ICS.

➡ **Set up your router/WAP to use the Internet:** You can adjust Internet connection settings, including setting a MAC address if your Internet Service Provider (ISP) requires you to use a specific one.

Get ready to . . .

Use the Windows Network Setup Wizard

1. Choose Start⇨All Programs⇨Accessories⇨ Communications⇨Network Setup Wizard.

2. In the resulting Network Setup Wizard, shown in Figure 2-1, click Next, read the on-screen instructions to connect all of your hardware, and then click Next again.

3. Choose whether or not you want your network to share an existing Internet connection. (You may be asked a different series of basic questions based on how you answer.)

4. When you see the screen shown in Figure 2-2, enter a description and name for the computer. Click Next.

    Give each computer a descriptive name, because this is how it will be identified to other computers on the network.

5. Enter a workgroup name. The workgroup name must be the same on every computer on the network.

6. Choose whether or not you want to allow file and printer sharing and click Next again.

    If you enable file and printer sharing, other people on your network can access shared folders and printers on your computer. If you choose not to enable file and printer sharing, the Windows XP Firewall prevents others from accessing items on your computer. I describe how to customize file and printer sharing in Chapter 4.

7. Review your settings in the next screen and click Next to apply them.

Figure 2-1: The Windows Network Setup Wizard.

 When the Network Setup Wizard is done, you will be asked if you want to create a network setup disk. Windows Network Setup disks uses floppy disks, so unless all of your computers have floppy drives creating a disk may not be very useful.

Figure 2-2: Enter a name and description for the computer.

Change the Workgroup Name

1. Open the Windows Control Panel and double-click the System icon to open it.

    You can also open System Properties by right-clicking the My Computer icon and choosing Properties from the menu that appears.

2. In the resulting System Properties dialog box, click the Computer Name tab (see Figure 2-3).

3. Click the Change button to open the Computer Name Changes dialog box.

4. Enter a new name in the Workgroup text box (see Figure 2-4).

    You can also change the computer's name in the Computer Name Changes dialog box.

5. Click OK to close each open dialog box.

    You should set the exact same workgroup name on each Windows PC on your network. If each PC doesn't have the same workgroup name, you won't be able to easily perform many networking tasks, such as printing and sharing files.

    If you change a computer's name or workgroup name, you must restart the computer for those changes to take effect.

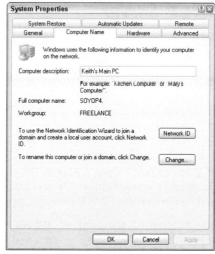

Figure 2-3: The Systems Properties dialog box, Computer Name tab.

Figure 2-4: The Computer Name Changes dialog box.

Set Up the DHCP Server in Your Router

1. Log in to the router using a Web browser and locate the DHCP controls.

   The DHCP controls are usually located on a General tab, or a special DHCP screen as shown in Figure 2-5.

2. Enable the DHCP server (see Figure 2-5). On D-Link routers, select the Enabled radio button. On some other routers, you need to choose the DHCP network type.

3. Choose a starting number for the range of IP addresses that you want the router to use.

4. Choose an ending number for the IP address range.

   Each computer on your network must have a unique IP address. If you know for sure that only four computers will ever access your network, you can limit the range of IP addresses to just four numbers by entering 100 as the starting number and 103 as the ending number. Doing so provides one additional level of security to your network.

5. Click OK or Apply to apply your changes. You may need to restart the router.

6. Reopen the DHCP controls and review the IP addresses assigned to each computer (see Figure 2-6).

   DHCP assigns IP addresses to computers that are turned on and connected to the network. Noting the IP addresses may come in handy later when troubleshooting network problems.

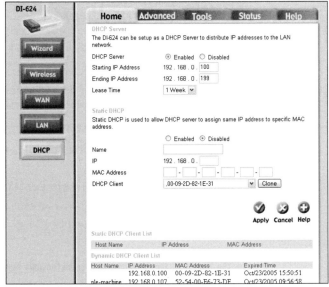

Figure 2-5: Enable the router's DHCP server.

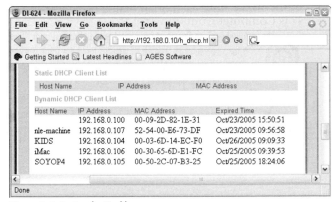

Figure 2-6: Review the IP addresses.

Share a Connection with Windows Internet Connection Sharing

1. On the computer that connects to the Internet, choose Start➪All Programs➪Accessories➪Communications➪ Network Setup Wizard to run the Windows Network Setup wizard.

 Only set up Internet Connection Sharing (ICS) if you connect to the Internet directly from a computer, such as through a dial-up modem. If you connect to the Internet through a broadband modem that is connected to a router, do not use ICS. Instead, use the router's built-in DHCP server as described in the previous task.

2. Click Next when the Network Setup Wizard begins, read the instructions on the screen shown in Figure 2-7, and click Next again.

3. Choose No, Let Me Choose Another Way to Connect to the Internet and click Next.

4. In the screen that appears (see Figure 2-8), select This Computer Connects Directly to the Internet and click Next.

5. In the resulting list of network cards and modems, select your modem and click Next.

 If your computer connects to the Internet using an external modem which is attached directly to your computer's network card, select the network card to which the modem is attached. The network card may actually be a USB port, depending on how you have your hardware set up.

6. Complete the Network Setup Wizard as I describe earlier in this chapter.

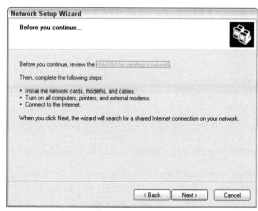

Figure 2-7: The Network Setup Wizard.

 When you set up ICS, your computer — called the host computer — becomes a DHCP server for the rest of the network. After the host is set up, the rest of the computers on your network must be set up as clients. Follow the instructions in the next two tasks to configure your other computers as DHCP clients. ICS clients can be other Windows PCs, or they can be Macintosh computers.

Figure 2-8: Set up ICS on the computer.

Configure a Windows PC as a DHCP Client

1. Open the Windows Control Panel and then double-click the Network Connections icon to open a list of network connections.

2. Double-click your current connection to the network.

3. In the resulting Status dialog box, click Properties.

4. In the Local Area Connection Properties dialog box, shown in Figure 2-9, select Internet Protocol (TCP/IP) and then click the Properties button.

5. In the Internet Protocol (TCP/IP) Properties dialog box (see Figure 2-10), select the Obtain an IP Address Automatically option.

6. Select the Obtain DNS server address automatically option.

7. Click OK and close all open dialog boxes.

 When you set your computer to obtain an IP address automatically, it gets the address from either your router's built-in DHCP server, or from an ICS Host on another computer. See the tasks in this chapter for setting up DHCP servers and ICS.

 You may need to restart your computer for your changes to take effect.

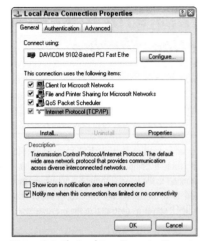

Figure 2-9: The Local Area Connection Properties dialog box.

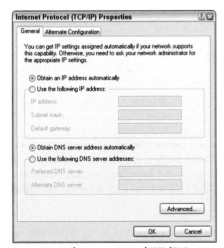

Figure 2-10: The Internet Protocol (TCP/IP) Properties dialog box.

Configure a Mac as a DHCP Client

1. Open System Preferences from the Apple menu and click the Network icon.

2. In the resulting Network control panel (see Figure 2-11), click the Show menu drop-down arrow and choose the network connection you use to connect to the network.

 If your computer connects to the network using the built-in Ethernet network port, choose Built-In Ethernet in the Show menu. If you connect using an AirPort Card, choose AirPort in the Show menu instead.

3. Click the TCP/IP tab (see Figure 2-12).

4. Click the Configure menu drop-down arrow and choose Using DHCP.

5. Click the Apply Now button and then close the Network control panel.

6. Press Command+Q to quit System Preferences and then restart your computer.

 If you're using a portable Mac, you can use it to connect to several different networks. For example, at home you may connect it to your home network using an Ethernet cable, but at Wi-Fi hotspots you may connect using AirPort instead. Use the Location menu at the top of the Network control panel to specify connection settings for different network locations.

 Macintosh OS X can obtain an IP address automatically from a DHCP server built in to any router, or from a Windows PC running Internet Connection Sharing.

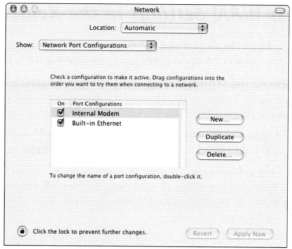

Figure 2-11: The Network control panel.

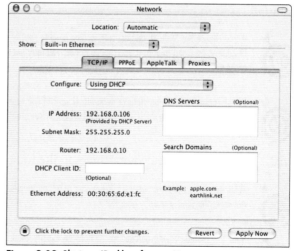

Figure 2-12: Obtain an IP address for your Mac.

Adjust WAN Settings in the Router

1. Log in to the router and locate the WAN controls on the General tab or a special WAN screen (see Figure 2-13).

2. Choose the setting that applies to your connection, as shown in Figure 2-14. Most WAN connections fall into one of three categories:

   - **Dynamic IP Address:** If you have a cable modem, you probably need to use the Dynamic IP address setting.

   - **Static IP Address:** Some Internet service providers (ISPs) assign static IP addresses to users. If you have a static IP address, choose the static option, as shown in Figure 2-13.

   - **PPPoE:** The Point-to-Point over Ethernet setting is most often used by DSL connections.

3. Enter additional connection information as required by your ISP.

If you choose the Static IP address setting, you need to specify the IP address assigned to you. If you choose PPPoE, you may need to enter your ISP account name and password.

PPPoE connections can be static or dynamic. If your PPPoE connection is static, also enter the IP address and DNS addresses provided by your ISP.

4. Click OK or Apply to save your changes in the router.

WAN stands for *wide area network*. When you're setting up a home network, the WAN is usually your ISP.

Your ISP should provide detailed instructions on exactly what settings to use in your router. The steps here should be considered guidelines that work in most cases, but if your ISP gives you special instructions you should follow those instead.

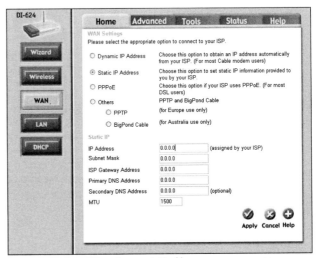

Figure 2-13: Some ISPs assign a static IP address.

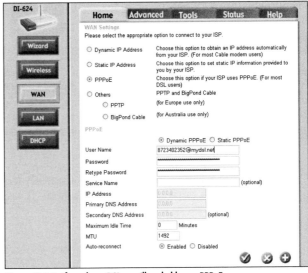

Figure 2-14: If you have DSL, you'll probably use PPPoE.

Clone Your PC's MAC Address

1. Log in to the router and locate the network activity log. (If you don't see a screen named Log, check the Status area.)

2. Write down the MAC address listed for your PC. (In Figure 2-15, MAC addresses are listed in the far-right column.)

3. Open the WAN settings in your router.

4. Enter the MAC address and click the Clone MAC Address button (see Figure 2-16). Your PC's MAC address has now been cloned to the router.

 Each network adapter connected to a network has a unique MAC (Media Access Control) address. Even game consoles, PDAs, and wireless cameras have unique MAC addresses.

 In most cases, you do not need to clone a MAC address. However, some ISPs register the MAC address of your computer, so if you change computers or add a router to your network your ISP may not let you online because the device now connected to the ISP has an unregistered MAC address. By cloning your PC's MAC address to your router, you avoid having to register a new MAC address with your ISP.

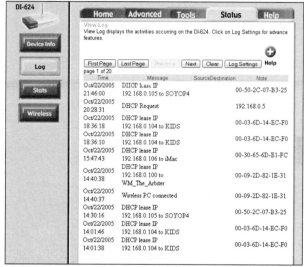

Figure 2-15: Find your MAC address.

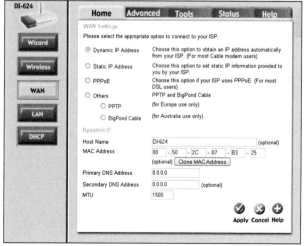

Figure 2-16: Clone the MAC address under WAN settings.

Adding Wireless Devices to Your Network

*A*fter you have a wireless access point (WAP) up and running, your next step is to add wireless devices to your network. To connect to your wireless network, computers and other network devices must meet two conditions:

➡ **Each device needs a wireless adapter.** Some of your devices — such as laptops — may already have built-in Wi-Fi capabilities. If not, you can install an internal Wi-Fi card or add an external Wi-Fi adapter.

➡ **Each wireless adapter must be configured for the network.** Each wireless device on your network must be able to find and access your WAP.

In this chapter, you find out how to add wireless computers to your network. I go over how to install the hardware and configure the software to make your wireless network function properly. I also describe how to find available Wi-Fi networks within range of your computer, a task that may come in handy if you visit a Wi-Fi hotspot. And you discover how to disable your computer's wireless adapter so that it doesn't automatically connect to wireless networks when you don't want it to happen.

Get ready to . . .

Install an Internal Wi-Fi Card

1. Follow the manufacturer's instructions to install the Wi-Fi card software.

    Make sure that you follow any special installation instructions provided by the Wi-Fi card's manufacturer. Most cards require you to install the supporting software before physically installing the card in your computer.

2. Leave the Wi-Fi card's installation CD-ROM in the CD-ROM drive and shut down your computer.

3. Disconnect all cables and move the case to a safe, clean working area.

4. Open the case of your computer as described in the manufacturer's documentation.

5. Locate an open PCI slot (see Figure 3-1).

6. Use a screwdriver to remove the blank-off plate on the back of the computer case next to the open PCI slot you plan to use.

7. Carefully insert the network card into the PCI slot.

8. Secure the card in the case, as shown in Figure 3-2.

9. Reconnect all cables and restart your computer.

Figure 3-1: Four empty PCI slots.

Figure 3-2: Secure the card in the case.

10. Log in to Windows

11. In the resulting Found New Hardware Wizard (see Figure 3-3), choose whether or not you want Windows Update to search for installation software for the card and then click Next.

 If the card's installation CD isn't still in the CD-ROM drive, insert it at this time. If you have the card's installation CD, choose No, not This Time in the Found New Hardware Wizard.

12. In the next screen, choose the Install the Software Automatically option and then click Next to install the driver.

 If you see a warning that the hardware hasn't passed Windows Logo testing, click Continue Anyway.

13. Click Finish to close the Found New Hardware Wizard.

 Warning: Computer hardware is very fragile. If you don't have experience installing expansion cards in computers or making other hardware upgrades, consider hiring a professional to install your Wi-Fi card. Computer retailers can install cards and other hardware you buy for a nominal fee.

Found New Hardware Wizard

Welcome to the Found New Hardware Wizard

Windows will search for current and updated software by looking on your computer, on the hardware installation CD, or on the Windows Update Web site (with your permission).

Read our privacy policy

Can Windows connect to Windows Update to search for software?

○ Yes, this time only
○ Yes, now and every time I connect a device
○ No, not this time

Click Next to continue.

< Back   Next >   Cancel

Figure 3-3: The Found New Hardware Wizard.

 After installing a new wireless networking card, visit the manufacturer's Web site (it should be listed in the card's documentation) and check its support pages for any updates for your card. It's possible that the card you bought sat on a store shelf for a couple of months, and during that time the manufacturer may have developed some important updates.

Connect an External Wi-Fi Adapter

1. Obtain an external adapter, such as the one shown in Figure 3-4, that is compatible with your computer.

    Most newer laptops have a cardbus slot that can accept a cardbus Wi-Fi adapter, as shown in Figure 3-4. Other wireless adapters can connect to a USB port or an Ethernet port.

2. Install the adapter's software as described by the manufacturer's documentation.

3. Connect the adapter to the appropriate port on your computer and then turn on the computer's power.

4. Follow the steps in the previous task to complete installation of the adapter's driver software.

    If you are using a cardbus-style Wi-Fi adapter in a laptop, remove the adapter when you are transporting the laptop. Leaving the adapter in the laptop's cardbus slot may damage it.

Figure 3-4: Cardbus Wi-Fi cards are compatible with most laptops.

 If you use a USB Wi-Fi adapter, make sure you connect it to a USB port directly on your computer, rather than a USB hub. Although connecting the adapter to a USB hub *might* work, the likelihood of configuration problems is greater.

 Some external Wi-Fi adapters connect to an Ethernet port on your computer, rather than a USB port or Cardbus slot. Adapters that use an Ethernet port are actually called network bridges because they create a bridge between an existing network connection and your network. See Chapter 16 for more on using network bridges.

Configure the Adapter Software

1. Double-click the desktop icon for the adapter software.

 In many cases, a Wi-Fi adapter's management software places an Icon In the Windows system tray, which is the area in the lower-right corner next to the clock. You should be able to double-click the system tray icon to open the adapter software.

2. When the program opens, locate the screen that lists available networks.

3. If your network appears in the list, select it. If your network doesn't appear, click Add under Preferred Networks.

4. Enter the SSID for your network and choose encryption settings that match the settings used in your WAP.

5. Enter the network key (see Figure 3-5).

6. Click OK and view your network in the Preferred networks list (see Figure 3-6). Click the Refresh button if your network does not appear in the list of available networks.

 In Chapter 6, I describe how to set the SSID, encryption, and network keys in your WAP. If you disable SSID broadcast as I recommend, the network will not be visible to your new wireless computer until you manually enter the SSID.

 Sometimes the Windows wireless connection utility does a better job of managing wireless connections than the software that comes with Wi-Fi cards. If you are unable to connect to your wireless network using the card's proprietary software, try using the Windows utility instead.

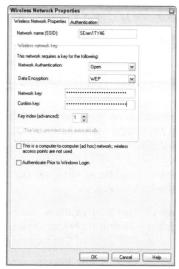

Figure 3-5: Set the SSID and network keys.

Figure 3-6: Check for available networks.

Start the Windows Wireless Connection Utility

1. Choose Start➪All Programs➪Accessories➪ Communications➪Network Connections.

    If your Wi-Fi card came with its own management software that is currently running on your computer, disable it before activating the Windows management utility.

2. In the resulting Network Connections window, double-click the Wireless Network Connection.

3. In the Wireless Network Connection window, click Set Up a Wireless Network for a Home or Small Office under Network Tasks on the left side of the window.

4. In the resulting Wireless Network Setup Wizard screen, click Next in the first screen of the wizard and then enter your network's SSID (see Figure 3-7).

5. If your network has a security key, choose whether it is assigned manually or automatically.

6. Select the WPA checkbox at the bottom of the screen if you use WPA encryption on your network. Click Next.

7. In the resulting screen, enter your network's security key if it's assigned manually, and then click Next again.

8. Select Set Up a Network Manually, click Next, and then click Finish. Your wireless network should now be active (see Figure 3-8).

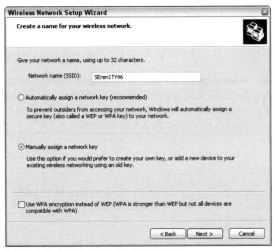

Figure 3-7: Enter the network's SSID.

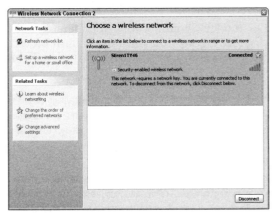

Figure 3-8: Your connection is now active.

Display the Wireless Connection System Tray Icon

1. Choose Start⇨All Programs⇨Accessories⇨ Communications⇨Network Connections.

2. In the Network Connections window, right-click your wireless connection and choose Properties from the resulting menu.

3. Select the Show Icon in Notification Area When Connected check box, as shown in Figure 3-9.

4. Click OK to close the Network Connection Properties dialog box.

5. Locate the wireless connection icon in the Windows system tray in the lower-right corner next to the clock, as shown in Figure 3-10.

 The system tray icon gives you quick access to settings for your wireless connection, which comes in handy when you need to manage your connection. Double-click the icon to open the Wireless Network Status window, or right-click the icon for additional options.

 Hover your mouse pointer over the wireless network system tray icon to quickly see the status of your wireless network. A tooltip appears, showing the wireless connection speed and signal quality.

Figure 3-9: Enable the system tray icon.

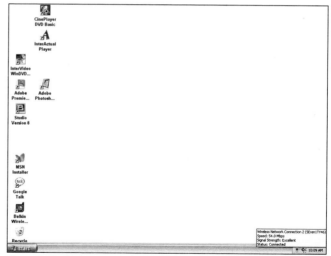

Figure 3-10: Check your network status.

Search for Wireless Networks

1. Double-click the wireless connection icon in the Windows system tray.

2. In the Wireless Network Connection Status dialog box, shown in Figure 3-11, click the View Wireless Networks button.

3. In the resulting Wireless Network Connection window, shown in Figure 3-12, click Refresh Network List in the Network Tasks menu on the left side of the screen.

 The system tray is the area in the lower-right corner of the screen, next to the clock. If you don't see a wireless connection icon there, see the previous task to enable the icon.

 Use the Wireless Network Connection window to manage your network connections. Using this window you can connect or disconnect from networks, or change the order of preferred networks when more than one is available.

Figure 3-11: Click View Wireless Networks.

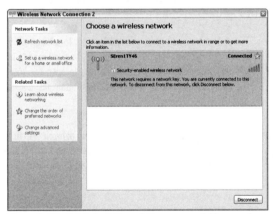

Figure 3-12: Click Refresh Network List to see available networks.

Disable the Wi-Fi Connection

1. Right-click the wireless connection icon in the Windows system tray, shown in Figure 3-13.

2. Choose Disable from the context menu that appears. The connection is disconnected, and the wireless connection icon disappears from the system tray.

 Right-clicking the wireless connection icon in the Windows system tray gives you access to several useful commands relating to the wireless connection. You can also use this context menu to quickly view a list of other available networks or to review the status of the connection.

 It's a good idea to disable your wireless connection if you are working in a remote location where other un-trusted wireless networks or computers may be active. Disabling your wireless connection prevents other networks and computers from accessing your computer.

Reactivate the Connection

1. Choose Start⇨Connect To.

2. In the submenu that appears, choose your wireless connection (see Figure 3-14). The connection is restored, and the wireless connection icon reappears in the Windows system tray.

 If you want to connect to a different network, choose Show All Connections from the Connect To menu. In the Network Connections window that appears, right-click the wireless connection and choose View Available Wireless Networks. You can then choose a different wireless network, if others are available.

Figure 3-13: Disable the connection.

Figure 3-14: Reconnect to your wireless network.

Choose a Network Access Mode

1. Double-click the wireless connection icon in the Windows system tray.

2. In the Wireless Network Connection Status dialog box, click the Properties button.

3. In the Wireless Network Connection Properties dialog box, click the Wireless Networks tab (see Figure 3-15).

4. Click the Advanced button to open the Advanced dialog box (see Figure 3-16).

5. Choose a network access mode:

   - **Any Available Network:** The computer tries to connect to any wireless network that is detected.

   - **Access Point (Infrastructure) Networks Only:** The computer tries to connect to networks using a wireless access point. This setting gives you more security, especially at Wi-Fi hotspots.

   - **Computer-to-Computer (ad hoc) Networks Only:** The computer tries to connect to other computers, called ad hoc networking. See Chapter 13 for more on using ad hoc networks.

6. If you want to automatically log on to any available wireless network, select the Automatically Connect to Non-Preferred Networks check box.

 Automatically logging on to any available network could leave your computer vulnerable to unknown and untrusted networks. Do not enable this option if your computer contains sensitive or personal information.

7. Click Close to close the Advanced dialog box and click OK to close all remaining dialog boxes.

Figure 3-15: Open the Wireless Networks tab.

Figure 3-16: Choose a network access mode.

Using Your Wireless Network

*C*hances are you have two main reasons for setting up a home network: you want to share an Internet connection between your computers and you want to be able to copy files between computers. I discuss how to share an Internet connection in Chapter 2, and in this chapter I cover how to share files. If you want to share files between your computers, you need to do the following:

→ **Share folders:** Computer files are organized into folders on your hard drive. In Windows and Mac OS X, access to those folders is strictly controlled. If you *own* a folder, other computers on your network — and even other users on the same computer — can't access it. To copy files back and forth over the network, you can *share* folders with others.

→ **Log in to other computers:** If your network is all Windows or all Macintosh, sharing files back and forth is easy. But if you have a mix of Windows PCs and Macs, you'll have to go through a special log in procedure before you can share files and folders.

→ **Transfer files:** Actually copying files across your network is the final step. I show you how to copy files between network computers, whether your computers are Windows PCs, Macs, or a mixture of both.

Get ready to . . .

Share a Folder in Windows

1. Choose Start➪All Programs➪Accessories➪
    Communications➪Network Connections.

2. In the Network Connections window, right-click your
    network connection and choose Properties from the
    menu that appears.

3. In the Network Connection Properties dialog box, select
    the File and Printer Sharing for Microsoft Networks
    check box, as shown in Figure 4-1.

> File and Printer Sharing may already be enabled on your com-
> puter, but you should double-check it to make sure.

4. Click OK to close the dialog box.

5. Open My Computer or Windows Explorer.

6. Locate the Shared Documents folder. Right-click the
    Shared Documents folder and choose Sharing and
    Security from the menu that appears.

7. In the resulting Properties dialog box, select the Share
    This Folder on the Network check box (see Figure 4-2).

8. Type a descriptive name for the folder in the Share
    Name field.

9. Click OK to close the Properties dialog box.

10. To share files or folders, copy them into the Shared
    Documents folder using My Computer or Windows
    Explorer.

> To create a new subfolder in the Shared Documents folder, open
> Shared Documents and then choose File➪New➪Folder. Give the
> new folder a descriptive name.

Figure 4-1: Enable File and Printer Sharing.

Figure 4-2: Share the folder.

Access a Shared Network Folder in Windows

1. Choose Start⇨My Network Places.

    You can also access My Network Places from My Computer or Windows Explorer. In My Computer, click My Network Places under Other Places on the left side of the screen. In Windows Explorer, click My Network Places near the bottom of the folder tree on the left side of the screen.

2. In the My Network Places window that appears, as shown in Figure 4-3, double-click the network place that you want to open.

    If you don't see a network folder that you think should be available, make sure that the computer containing the network folder is turned on and connected to the network. Also, double-check the file sharing settings on the other computer as described in the previous task.

3. Browse the network folder (see Figure 4-4).

4. To copy an item to a shared network folder, simply click and drag it to the shared folder's window.

    You can also use Cut, Copy, and Paste commands when browsing shared network drives.

    When you share a folder, anyone on your network can access it. Do not store private or sensitive files in shared folders.

Figure 4-3: Choose a network place.

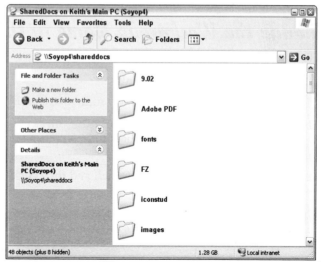

Figure 4-4: Browse the folder.

Enable File Sharing in OS X

1. Open System Preferences from the Apple menu and then click Sharing.

2. In the resulting Sharing control panel (see Figure 4-5), provide a descriptive name for your computer. (Other computers will see this name over the network.)

3. Select the Personal File Sharing check box. If you will be sharing folders with Windows PCs, check the Windows File Sharing option as well.

4. Close the Sharing control panel.

These steps assume that you have Mac OS Version 10.2 or better. If you have an earlier version of the Macintosh operating system, I strongly recommend that you upgrade. Windows File Sharing is only available in Mac OS 10.2 or better. Sharing files between Windows and older versions of Mac OS require special third-party programs.

Change the Workgroup Name in OS X

1. Open the Applications folder on your hard drive and then open the Utilities subfolder.

2. Double-click the Directory Access utility to open it.

3. Click the lock icon at the bottom of the Directory Access utility and then enter an administrator name and password.

4. Select SMB/CIFS on the Services tab and then click the Configure button.

5. Enter your Windows workgroup name in the Workgroup field (see Figure 4-6) and click OK.

Figure 4-5: The Sharing control panel.

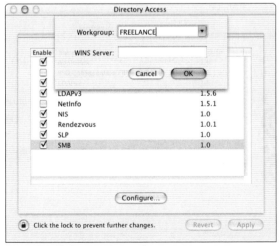

Figure 4-6: The Directory Access utility.

Create a Windows User Account

1. Open System Preferences from the Apple menu.

2. Click the Accounts icon to open the Accounts window.

3. Click New User (OS 10.3 and earlier) or the plus sign in the lower-left corner of the Accounts window (OS 10.4 and later).

4. Enter a name, short name, and password for the user (see Figure 4-7).

    I recommend naming the account Windows to help you remember the purpose of the account later.

5. Select the Allow User to Log In from Windows check box if you see it.

   As the name implies, this option enables users to log in using this account on Windows PCs. This option is not available (or required) in newer versions of Mac OS X.

6. Click Save or Create Account (depending on your OS X version) to save the new user account. The Windows account now appears in the list of user accounts, as shown in Figure 4-8.

   Because Mac OS X is based on UNIX, user account names and passwords are case sensitive. Make sure that Windows users on your network know this, because if the user name is "Windows" and they try to log on using "windows," the log in attempt will be unsuccessful.

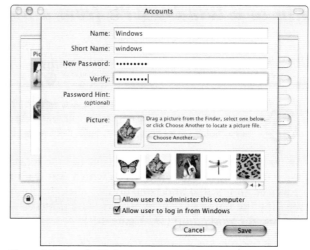

Figure 4-7: Name the Windows user account.

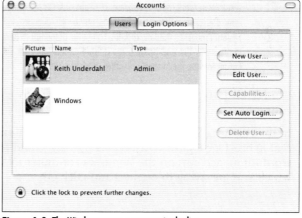

Figure 4-8: The Windows account appears in the list.

Log In to a Windows PC from a Mac

1. In Mac OS 10.2 or 10.3, choose Go⇨Connect to Server. In OS 10.4 and later, open Finder and then click Network.

   You may need to wait several seconds for the list of computers to be populated. In some cases you may also see a Windows workgroup name listed. If you see the workgroup, double-click it to open it.

2. In the Connect to Server window (OS 10.2 or 10.3), click the name of the computer to which you want to connect. In OS 10.4 and later, double-click the folder bearing the name of your Windows workgroup to browse the workgroup (see Figure 4-9).

   By default, newer Macs are set with the default workgroup name "Workgroup." This probably isn't the correct workgroup name for your Windows workgroup. To check the workgroup name for your Windows network, go to a Windows PC, right-click the My Computer icon, and choose Properties from the menu that appears. In the System Properties window, click the Computer Name tab to bring it to the front. The workgroup name is listed on this tab. Click OK or Cancel to close the System Properties window.

3. Double-click the computer to which you want to connect.

4. In the resulting SMB/CIFS Filesystem Authentication dialog box (see Figure 4-10), type a username and password for an account on the Windows computer to which you are trying to connect and click OK.

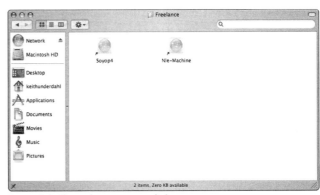

Figure 4-9: Choose the computer to which you want to connect.

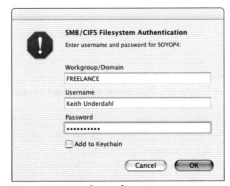

Figure 4-10: Enter log in information.

If you only want to access shared items on the Windows PC, just enter any user name and leave the password field empty. Doing so gives you access to public items on the Windows PC.

5. Choose a volume that you want to mount (see Figure 4-11).

 Items in the list of things you can mount include shared folders, as well as folders owned by the user account you are using to log in to the Windows PC.

6. Click OK. The selected item mounts on your computer as if it were a disk drive or volume.

7. Double-click the network volume's desktop icon to browse its contents (see Figure 4-12).

 In Mac OS 10.4 and later, you can also access mounted volumes directly from Finder. In the Finder window, simply click the volume's icon in the upper-left corner.

8. Click and drag files to copy them between computers.

 If you only want to access shared folders on the Windows PC, enter any user name in Step 4 and leave the password blank. You will still be able to log in to the Windows PC, although you will only be able to access shared folders.

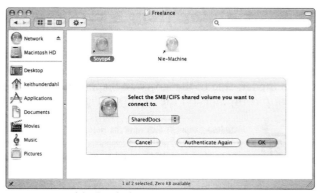

Figure 4-11: Find the shared volume.

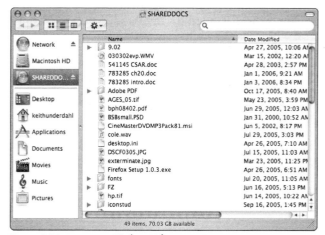

Figure 4-12: Browse your Windows PC from your Mac.

Log In to a Mac from a Windows PC

1. Open My Network Places from the Windows Start menu.

2. Click View Workgroup Computers under Network Tasks on the left side of the screen to display the list of workgroup computers on the right (see Figure 4-13).

 Macintosh computers may have the word Samba in front of their names in the list of workgroup computers. Samba is the Mac OS X software that allows Windows and Macintosh PCs to network with each other.

3. Double-click a Macintosh computer in the list.

4. In the resulting Connect To dialog box, enter the user name and password for the Windows user account on the Mac, as shown in Figure 4-14.

5. Click OK to log in. After you are logged in, you can see a list of available files and folders on the Mac.

 You can only access items that are owned by the Windows user account on the Mac. If you want to share items with other user accounts on the Mac, store them in the Public folder. Each user's Public folder in Mac OS X is shared with other users.

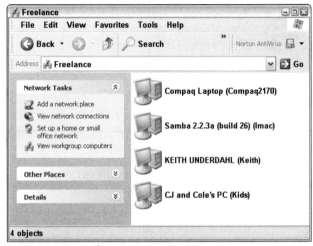

Figure 4-13: View workgroup computers.

Figure 4-14: Log in to the Mac from Windows.

Copy Files Between Networked Macs

1. In Mac OS 10.4 and later, double-click your hard drive icon to open Finder. In older versions of Mac OS X, Choose Go⇨Connect to Server and skip ahead to Step 3.

 You can also open Finder from the Dock.

2. In Finder, click Network.

 If you don't see your other Mac listed in the network window, open the My Network folder. If you have Windows PCs on your network, you may also be able to access other Macs through the folder for your Windows workgroup.

3. Double-click the computer to which you want to connect, as shown in Figure 4-15 (OS 10.4 and later) or Figure 4-16 (OS 10.3 and earlier).

4. In the login box that appears (OS 10.4 and later shown in Figure 4-15), log in using one of the following options:

- **Guest:** If you log in as a guest, no user name or password is required. You will only be able to access public folders on the network computer.

- **Registered User:** You must enter a valid user name and password for a user account on the network computer. When you log in as a registered user, you can access that user's files and folders.

5. Click the Connect button.

6. In the dialog box that appears, choose a volume that you want to mount and click OK.

Figure 4-15: Log in from OS 10.4 and later.

 After you connect, you will see an icon for the network computer on your desktop. Double-click this icon to access the network computer.

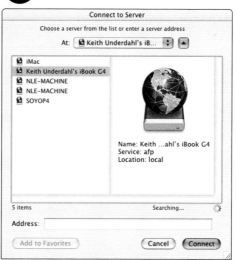

Figure 4-16: Log in from older versions of OS X.

Wireless Networking with Your Mac

*W*indows PCs aren't the only computers that can take advantage of Wi-Fi networks. Macintosh computers have been at the forefront of wireless networking with AirPort, Apple's name for the Wi-Fi technology used in modern Macs. Most new Macs have AirPort Extreme — a newer, faster version of AirPort — built right in, and even if you buy a new Mac without AirPort Extreme you may be able to install a card. By using AirPort or AirPort Extreme, you can connect your Mac to any 802.11b/g Wi-Fi network.

In this chapter, I discuss how to use AirPort to connect your Mac to Wi-Fi networks, whether at home or at a hotspot. If your computer doesn't already have AirPort, I show you how to install an AirPort Extreme card in your Mac. Before you buy an AirPort Extreme card, however, make sure that your computer is AirPort Extreme-ready. If you're not sure that your Mac is compatible, visit `http://docs.info.apple.com/article.html?artnum=107440`.

 Some Macs — such as the Mac mini — can only be upgraded by an Apple repair professional. When you buy a new Mac, spend a little extra money to get an AirPort Extreme card preinstalled — it's worth it.

Chapter 5

Get ready to . . .

Install an AirPort Card in an iBook

1. Shut down your iBook and remove the battery.

    To remove the battery, use a coin to turn the lock screw on the bottom of the iBook to the unlocked position.

2. On the front of your iBook, push the keyboard release tabs (see Figure 5-1) towards the front of the iBook and gently lift the keyboard out of the chassis.

    You don't need to disconnect the keyboard; simply rest it upside down on the touch pad.

3. Locate the built-in AirPort antenna in the space provided for the AirPort card (see Figure 5-2).

    If you don't see a space for the AirPort card, as shown in Figure 5-2, your iBook either is not compatible with AirPort or it already has AirPort installed.

4. Connect the antenna to the antenna port on the AirPort card.

5. Insert the AirPort card into the slot, ensuring that the connector pins seat firmly in the AirPort card socket.

    Do not force the card into position. If the AirPort card and the port on your computer don't match, you probably have the wrong kind of card for your iBook model.

6. Seat the AirPort card wire retention clasp and replace the keyboard and battery.

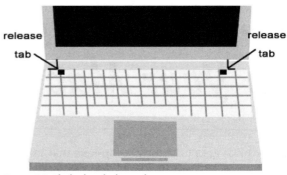

Figure 5-1: The keyboard release tabs.

Figure 5-2: The AirPort card slot under the keyboard.

Install an AirPort Card in an eMac

1. Open the DVD-ROM disc tray and leave it open.

2. Shut down your computer and make sure that the power is off.

    Disconnect the power cable to make sure that the computer doesn't accidentally turn on while you are installing the card.

3. Remove the two Philips-head screws on the cover inside the disc tray to reveal the AirPort card slot (see Figure 5-3).

4. Disconnect the antenna from the cover and then press the antenna into the AirPort card's antenna port.

5. Insert the AirPort card firmly into the slot until it seats and then reinstall the cover inside the disc tray.

Update AirPort Software

1. Make sure that your Mac can connect to the Internet using a wired solution, such as a direct connection to a modem or an Ethernet cable, to network with a shared connection.

    See Chapter 2 for more on using a shared Internet connection with your Mac.

2. Turn on your Mac and choose Apple➪Software Update to run the Software Update (see Figure 5-4).

3. Download and install any necessary updates to your computer that are identified by Software Update.

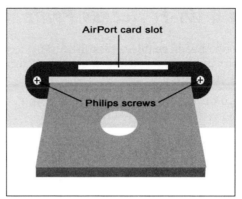

Figure 5-3: The AirPort card slot.

Figure 5-4: Check for updates.

Connect to a Wi-Fi Access Point

1. If AirPort isn't already enabled, click the AirPort icon on the menu bar in the upper-right corner of the screen and choose Turn AirPort On.

2. Click the AirPort icon in the menu bar again and choose Other to connect to a new Wi-Fi network.

 If the access point is set to broadcast its SSID, it may appear in the list of available networks in the AirPort menu. If you see the network to which you want to connect listed, click its name.

3. In the resulting Closed Network dialog box (see Figure 5-5), enter the network's SSID in the Network Name text box.

4. Choose a Wireless Security method as needed for the network.

 I show how to change WEP and WPA-PSK keys later in this chapter.

5. Click OK to connect to the network.

6. Check the status and signal strength of the Wi-Fi network by clicking the AirPort icon in the menu bar and choosing Open Internet Connect (see Figure 5-6).

Figure 5-5: Enter the network's SSID.

Figure 5-6: Check signal strength and status.

Manage Wi-Fi Networks

1. Choose Apple⇨System Preferences to open the System Preferences window.

2. Click the Network icon to open the Network dialog box.

3. Choose AirPort in the Show menu to reveal AirPort settings (see Figure 5-7).

4. In the By Default, Join menu, choose Preferred Networks.

5. In the resulting list, rearrange the order by clicking and dragging networks up or down in the list (see Figure 5-8).

    AirPort attempts to connect with the network at the top of the list first, and then moves down the list in order.

6. To remove a network from the list, click the network to select it and then click the Remove (-) button.

7. Select a network and choose Edit to change encryption keys and other network details for a given network.

8. When you are done making changes, click the Apply Now button and then quit System Preferences.

Figure 5-7: Choose AirPort in the Show menu.

Figure 5-8: Networks at the top of the list are most preferred.

Set Up WEP Encryption

1. Choose Apple⇨System Preferences to open the System Preferences window.

2. Click the Network icon to open the Network dialog box.

3. Choose AirPort in the Show menu and choose Preferred Networks in the By Default, Join menu.

4. Select a network in the list of networks and click Edit.

5. In the Wireless Security menu, choose a WEP option, as shown in Figure 5-9. Choose ASCII or HEX as appropriate for your network.

 If you're not sure whether to choose ASCII or HEX, or if your network uses 64-bit WEP encryption, choose WEP Password instead.

6. Enter the WEP key in the password text box shown in Figure 5-10.

7. Click OK and then quit Network Preferences.

 To make sure you're typing the WEP key correctly, temporarily select the Show Password check box so that you can see the characters you are typing. Make sure no one is looking over your shoulder when you do this.

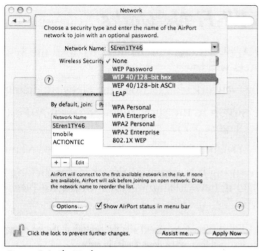

Figure 5-9: The Wireless security menu.

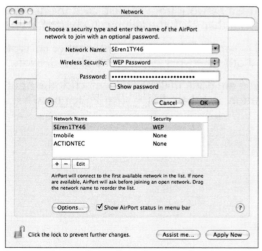

Figure 5-10: Enter the WEP key in the Password text box.

Configure WPA Encryption

1. Choose Apple⇨System Preferences to open the System Preferences window.

2. Click the Network icon to open the Network dialog box.

3. Choose AirPort in the Show drop-down menu and choose Preferred Networks in the By Default, Join menu.

4. Select a network in the list of networks and click Edit.

5. In the Wireless Security menu, choose WPA Personal, as shown in Figure 5-11.

> WPA Personal is equivalent to WPA-PSK, which is used by many wireless access points. WPA Enterprise requires that a RADIUS server be running on your network, something your home network is not likely to have.

6. Enter the WPA password in the password text box shown in Figure 5-12.

7. Click OK and then quit Network Preferences.

> WPA encryption is much more secure than WEP encryption. You should use WPA-PSK/WPA Personal encryption on your home wireless network unless you have computers that only support WEP.

Figure 5-11: Choose WPA Personal.

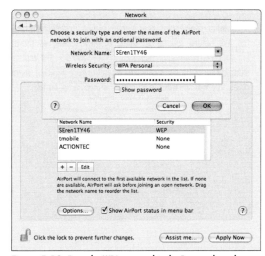

Figure 5-12: Enter the WPA password in the Password text box.

Disable AirPort

1. Click the AirPort icon in the menu bar and choose Turn AirPort Off, as shown in Figure 5-13.

    You should disable AirPort whenever you are not using it, especially when you are working in a public area. Leaving AirPort enabled allows others to potentially access your computer.

2. Choose Apple⇨System Preferences.

3. Click the Network icon in System Preferences to open the Network settings window, and then choose AirPort in the Show menu.

4. In the resulting AirPort settings, click the Options button.

5. Select automatic connection options, as shown in Figure 5-14.

    To maintain control over your wireless network connections, choose the Ask Before Joining an Open Network option, as shown in Figure 5-14. When you choose this option, AirPort asks you if you want to connect to open networks when they are detected. In many cases, you will not want to join open, unknown networks.

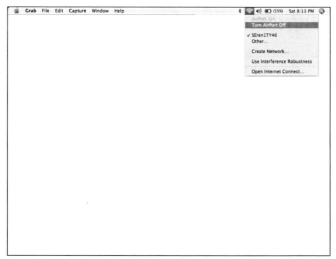

Figure 5-13: Disable wireless networking.

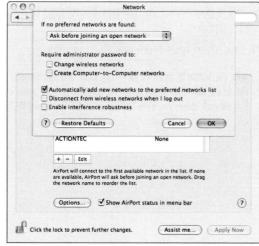

Figure 5-14: Connection options.

Part II
Securing Your Network

The 5th Wave   By Rich Tennant

"Frankly, the idea of an entirely wireless future scares me to death."

Activating Wi-Fi Security

*W*i-Fi technologies bring new levels of ease and convenience to home computer networking. No longer do you have to run Ethernet cable all over your house or confine computers to a single room. With Wi-Fi you can use your computers anywhere — even the backyard on a sunny day — that gets reception from your wireless access point (WAP).

Of course, the convenience of Wi-Fi brings with it a new security threat. Anyone within broadcast range of your wireless network signal — neighbors, passers-by — can access your network. After they have access to the network, they can steal your Internet bandwidth, view your sensitive computer files, and even damage your software and operating system. No matter where your network is located, you should take some basic precautions to keep it secure.

In this chapter, you find out how to start securing your wireless network. I go over how to determine your security threats, and what you need to do to protect yourself from them. I also show you how to activate security features in your wireless access point.

 I show how to implement various security measures in this chapter, including WEP encryption, WPA-PSK encryption, and MAC filtering. Of these methods, WPA-PSK provides the greatest level of security and should be used whenever possible. Only use WEP and MAC filtering if some of your wireless devices don't support WPA-PSK.

Get ready to . . .

Determine the Level of Security You Need

1. Decide whether or not you want others to be able to easily use your Wi-Fi network periodically.

    If you want to create a hotspot that friends or associates can use, you will want to use minimal security so that others can easily access it.

2. Walk around your building, property, and general area with your handheld PC or laptop to measure the range of your Wi-Fi signal in different areas (see Figure 6-1).

3. Evaluate the proximity of potential threats.

4. Find out what your equipment supports. In Figure 6-2, this router supports several encryption technologies including:

   - **WEP (Wireless Encryption Protocol):** WEP is supported by virtually all Wi-Fi devices. Unfortunately WEP is easily defeated by widely available hacking programs.

   - **WPA (Wi-Fi Protected Access):** WPA is vastly superior to WEP, but it requires a special RADIUS server, which most home networks don't have.

   - **WPA-PSK (WPA Pre-Shared Key):** This option is a form of WPA that does not require a RADIUS server and is the best choice for home networks. WPA-PSK is also called WPA Personal. Some older devices don't support WPA or WPA-PSK.

5. Routinely check for Wi-Fi intrusions. (I go over how to check for and eject unauthorized users in Chapter 8.)

Figure 6-1: A weak signal.

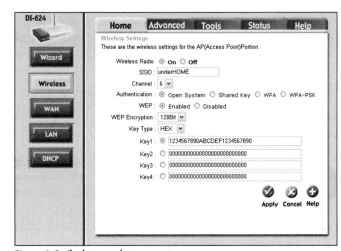

Figure 6-2: Check to see what your equipment supports.

Disable SSID Broadcast

1. Log in to the control panel for your WAP using a Web browser. (For just the steps to do so, refer to Chapter 1.)

2. Locate the SSID broadcast controls, usually found in the wireless controls area. (On some routers, such as the one shown in Figure 6-3, SSID broadcast controls are located on the Performance tab of the Advanced tab.)

3. Select the Disabled radio button next to SSID Broadcast.

4. Click OK or Apply to save your changes in the access point.

 The SSID (short for *service set identifier*) is the digital name of your wireless network, and it is the first layer of security for your network. If a wireless device wants to access your network, it must first know the correct SSID. If a laptop, PDA, game console, or other wireless device doesn't know the correct SSID, it can't log on to your network. Unfortunately, if your access point is broadcasting the SSID, then you lose this security layer because others can easily see your network, and they know the correct SSID.

5. Use a wireless computer that has not yet been set up to access your network to check for SSID broadcast, as shown in Figure 6-4. If SSID broadcast is disabled, your network should not be detected.

 If SSID broadcast has been enabled on your access point, change the SSID after you disable SSID broadcast. If someone detected your SSID before you disabled broadcast, they probably still have it saved in their list of available networks.

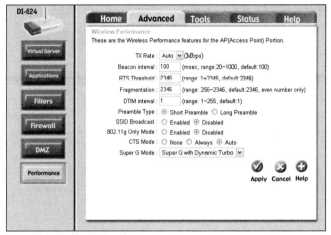

Figure 6-3: Disable SSID broadcast.

Figure 6-4: I've found a wireless network named tmobile.

Filter MAC Addresses

1. Determine the MAC address for each wireless computer and device on your network. (For just the steps to do so, turn to Chapter 8.)

2. Log in to the control panel for your WAP using a Web browser.

3. Locate the MAC filter controls. Most routers have a special Filters screen (see Figure 6-5).

4. If the router offers both IP and MAC filtering, select MAC Filters.

5. Select the Only Allow filtering option.

 When you choose the Only Allow option, only computers with the MAC addresses you enter will be allowed on your network by the router.

6. Enter the MAC address for one of your computers. Make sure that the first MAC address you enter is the one for the computer from which you are currently working.

 In many routers, you can use the DHCP pull-down menu to select computers that are currently connected to the network, and then click the Clone button to automatically fill in the Name and MAC Address fields. Doing this saves you some typing.

7. Enter a name for the computer so that it can be easily identified later.

8. Click Apply to apply the filter.

9. Repeat the above steps until all of your computers are entered (see Figure 6-6).

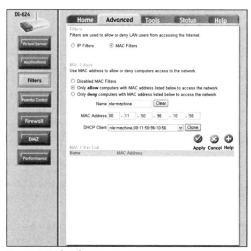

Figure 6-5: The Filters screen.

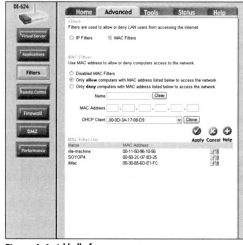

Figure 6-6: Add all of your computers.

Activate WEP Encryption

1. Log in to the control panel for your WAP using a Web browser.

2. Locate the wireless security controls in your access point (see Figure 6-7).

3. Enable WEP encryption and set the following options:

   - **Bit Depth:** Choose the highest possible setting, which is normally 128-bit.

   - **Key Type:** Choose HEX (hexadecimal) or ASCII. Some wireless devices can only use hexadecimal keys.

4. Enter at least one key and click OK or Apply to apply your changes.

Change the WEP Key

1. Log in to the control panel for your WAP using a Web browser.

2. Locate the wireless security controls in your access point.

3. Enter a new key in the access point and then click OK or Apply to apply the new key in the WAP.

4. Open the connection utility in your wireless device. (For just the steps to do so, refer to Chapter 3.)

5. Enter the WEP key in the wireless device (see Figure 6-8) and click OK or Apply to apply your new key.

 WEP keys are not case sensitive, however, when you set a hexa-decimal WEP key you can only use digits 0–9 and letters A–F. A 128-bit WEP key is 26 characters long.

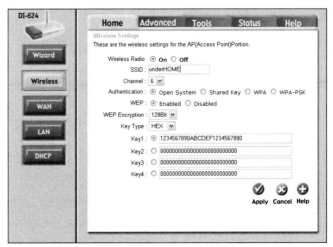

Figure 6-7: Enable WEP encryption.

Figure 6-8: Enter the WEP key in your wireless device.

Rotate Multiple WEP Keys

1. Log in to the control panel for your WAP using a Web browser.

2. Locate the wireless security controls in your access point.

3. Enter up to four unique WEP keys, as shown in Figure 6-9.

4. Select which key you want to use today and click OK or Apply to apply your new key.

5. Open the connection utility in your wireless device.

6. Click the arrows next to the Key Index box to choose Key Index 1, 2, 3, or 4 (see Figure 6-10).

7. Enter the WEP key matching the Key Index number.

8. Repeat Steps 6 and 7 for each Key Index.

9. Select the currently active Key Index and click OK to close the connection utility.

 By using multiple WEP keys and rotating them frequently — for example, once daily or every other day — you greatly increase the security of your network. Hackers need a lot of time to detect and decrypt a single WEP key, and multiple keys increase that challenge exponentially. Rotating WEP keys provides a way to slightly enhance your network security if your hardware doesn't allow you to use WPA-PSK encryption.

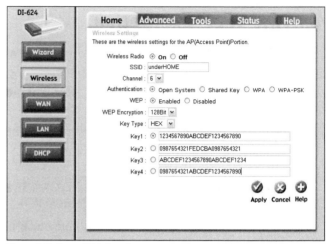

Figure 6-9: Use muiltiple keys for greater security.

Figure 6-10: Choose a Key Index.

Enhance Security with WPA-PSK Encryption

1. Log in to the control panel for your WAP using a Web browser.

2. Locate the wireless security controls in your access point.

3. Select WPA-PSK as the authentication method.

4. Enter a passphrase in both Passphrase boxes (see Figure 6-11).

 The passphrase can be between 8 and 63 characters, and it can include symbols such as question marks and ampersands. The passphrase should be long, random, and include both letters and numbers.

5. Click OK or Apply to apply your changes.

6. If your network has a RADIUS server, select WPA, as shown in Figure 6-12. Enter the IP address, Port number, and Shared secret for your RADIUS server.

 RADIUS servers are usually only found in corporate networks.

 WPA-PSK stands for Wi-Fi Protected Access Pre-Shared Key (WPA-PSK), and is more secure than WEP encryption. The only disadvantage of WPA-PSK is that it is not supported by some older Wi-Fi gear.

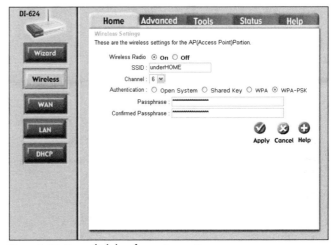

Figure 6-11: Use muiltiple keys for greater security.

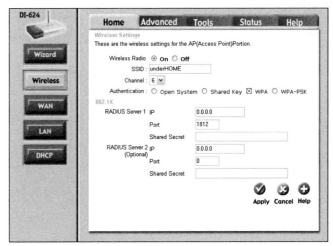

Figure 6-12: WPA requires a RADIUS server.

Update the WPA-PSK Key in Your Wireless Devices

1. Open the connection utility in your wireless device.

2. Locate the network security controls.

3. In the Network Authentication drop-down list, choose WPA-PSK.

 If your connection utility allows you to choose the TKIP or AES encryption methods, choose TKIP.

4. Enter the Network key (see Figure 6-13).

5. Click OK to apply your changes.

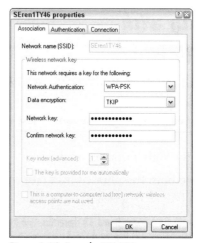

Figure 6-13: Enter the WPA-PSK.

Managing Firewalls and Network Security

Your home network faces a variety of security threats. These threats can be divided into two categories:

➡ **Wireless intrusion:** Wireless intrusion comes from other people within radio broadcast range of your wireless access point. Wireless intrusion generally comes from people who are physically close to you, at a distance usually less than 100 meters. Chapter 6 shows you how to activate wireless encryption to protect against Wi-Fi intruders.

➡ **Internet intrusion:** Hackers create programs that can enter your network through your Internet connection. They can access your files and personal information, and possibly change settings or damage your operating system so that you can't use your computer. The risk of Internet intrusion is even greater if you have an always-on broadband Internet connection, such as DSL or cable. Internet intrusion can come from down the block or halfway around the world.

The best protection from Internet-based intruders is having a firewall program. Just as firewalls in cars and office buildings prevent the spread of fire, firewall programs provide a protective barrier between your computer and the denizens of the Internet. This chapter shows you how to set up and use firewalls to protect your computers and your network.

Get ready to . . .

Configure the Windows Firewall

1. Choose Start⇨Control Panel to open the Windows Control Panel.

2. Double-click the Security Center icon.

    The Security Center icon is only available if you have Windows XP SP2 or better installed. If you don't see the Security Center icon in your Windows XP Control Panel, use Windows Update to download and install the SP2 update.

3. In the resulting Windows Security Center window (see Figure 7-1), click the Windows Firewall link.

4. In the resulting Windows Firewall dialog box, click the General tab and select the On radio button, as shown in Figure 7-2.

    You should only run one software firewall on a computer. If you have a third-party firewall program such as Norton Internet Security, ZoneAlarm, or a similar program, you may want to disable the Windows Firewall and use the more powerful third-party program instead.

    If you are using your computer at a public Wi-Fi hotspot, select the Don't Allow Exceptions check box. When you enable the Don't Allow Exceptions option, you can use Web browsers and e-mail programs, but you cannot use Internet messaging programs, FTP programs, and other programs which must access the Internet. Disallowing such programs protects your computer from being accessed by other people at the hotspot.

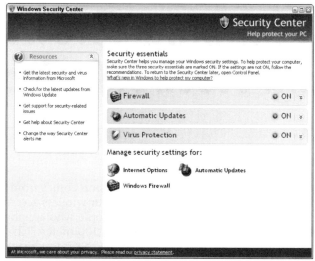

Figure 7-1: The Windows Security Center.

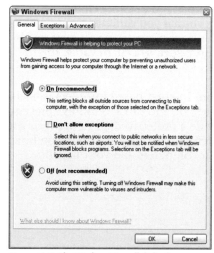

Figure 7-2: The Windows Firewall dialog box.

5. Click the Advanced tab (see Figure 7-3).

6. Review the network connections to which the Windows Firewall is applied and select or deselect them as needed.

> Normally you should leave all network connections checked, as shown in Figure 7-3. However, if you have trouble using devices (other than networking devices) that are connected to your IEEE-1394 port, you may want to uncheck 1394 Connection. This connection will not be listed if your computer doesn't have an IEEE-1394 (also called *FireWire*) port.

7. Click the Settings button in the Security Logging area.

8. In the resulting Log Settings dialog box, select both the Log Dropped Packets and Log Successful Connections check boxes, as shown in Figure 7-4.

> By logging dropped packets you may be able to determine whether network problems are due to a poor Wi-Fi signal. Lots of dropped packets may indicate a poor or intermittent signal. Logging successful connections can also help you troubleshoot connection issues; if you don't see any successful connections in the log, then you know that you aren't connecting to the network. I show how to review logs later in this chapter.

9. Click OK to close the Log Settings dialog box.

10. Click OK to close the Windows Firewall dialog box.

> If you have a router between your broadband Internet modem and the rest of your network, that router should also have a built-in firewall. This built-in firewall serves as a great first line of defense to your network, but it does not take the place of software firewalls installed on each computer on your network.

Figure 7-3: Advanced Windows Firewall settings.

Figure 7-4: The Log Settings dialog box.

Set Up a Third-Party Firewall

1. Open the Windows Firewall controls and select the Off radio button.

   > The Windows Firewall is likely to conflict with third-party firewall programs, thus preventing you from accessing the Internet.

2. Install the third-party firewall in accordance with the instructions provided by the program's publisher.

3. Open the firewall's control panel by double-clicking its icon in the Windows system tray (see Figure 7-5).

   > Many programs now market themselves as antivirus and Internet security programs. A program that is marketed as an Internet security program should include a firewall feature.

4. In the security program's control panel, locate the firewall controls. Make sure that the firewall is enabled.

   > The firewall controls may be labeled *Personal Firewall* and may be a subcategory of general network controls.

5. If the program offers security profiles, choose the profile that seems to best describe your network, as I have done (see Figure 7-6).

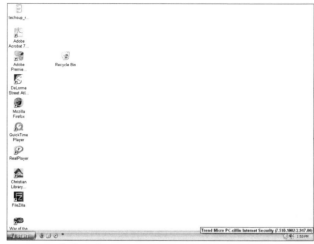

Figure 7-5: The firewall program's system tray icon.

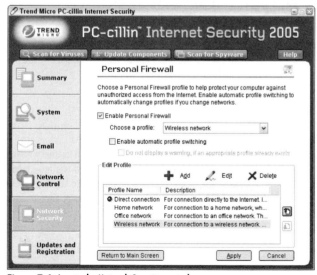

Figure 7-6: Locate the Network Security controls.

6. Choose a profile and then click Edit.

 These steps are for the Trend Micro security program shown in Figure 7-6, but most security programs should let you review and edit settings for the various security profiles that are available.

7. In the profile settings that appear, check the security level for the profile (see Figure 7-7).

 Carefully review the security settings for every profile because they may hold surprises. For example, the Trend Micro Home Network profile has the security level set to Low, as opposed to Medium, which I recommend.

8. Close the firewall program and save your settings.

 Make sure that when you close the program, the program's icon is still in the Windows system tray. If the icon is present, the program is still running.

Update the Firewall

1. Right-click the firewall program's icon in the Windows system tray.

2. In the context menu (see Figure 7-8), choose Update Components.

3. Follow the on-screen instructions to download and install updates.

 Most firewall programs automatically check for updates on a regular basis; if it has been a couple of days since you saw an update being performed, perform a manual update.

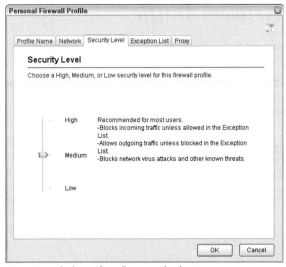

Figure 7-7: Check your firewall's security level.

Figure 7-8: Update your firewall.

Halt Network Traffic

1. Right-click the Windows system tray icon for your Internet security program.

2. In the context menu, choose Halt Internet Traffic, as shown in Figure 7-9. Traffic between your computer and the Internet should be disabled.

 The Halt Internet Traffic command can be used as an emergency panic button if you believe that your computer is currently under attack. For example, if your computer is currently having a lot of hard drive activity but no programs are running, and your Internet connection is flowing a lot of data but no one is online, activate the Halt Internet Traffic command. If the hard drive activity or connection activity suddenly stops, then it is likely that your computer was being attacked.

3. Run a complete virus and Internet security scan of your computer to identify and neutralize potential threats on your computer.

4. Choose Halt Internet Traffic again to re-enable Internet traffic. You can also disable and enable traffic from directly within your security program, as shown in Figure 7-10.

 The Halt Internet Traffic command only works on the computer on which it is installed. Halting Internet traffic on one computer won't prevent other computers on your network from connecting with the Internet.

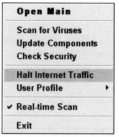

Figure 7-9: Halt Internet traffic.

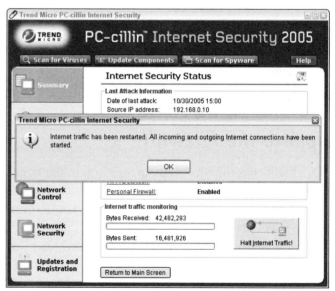

Figure 7-10: Reactivate your Internet connection when you believe it's safe.

Review the Firewall Logs

1. Open the control panel for your firewall program.

2. Locate the logging or event logs section of the control panel and open it.

3. Open a log:

- **Third-Party Firewalls:** If the program maintains several different kinds of logs, choose the Firewall or Personal Firewall logs and click View Logs.

- **Windows Firewall:** Use My Computer or Windows Explorer to open the folder C:\WINDOWS and then double-click the file pfirewall.log.

4. Review the firewall logs (see Figure 7-11). If you are using the Windows Firewall, the file pfirewall.log opens in a text editor (see Figure 7-12).

 When you review the firewall logs, look for entries that come from source IP addresses outside of your network. Sources inside your own network usually start with 192.168, as shown in Figures 7-11 and 7-12.

 Most activities listed in the firewall logs are harmless network functions. However, if you are having network connection difficulties, or if you have been victimized by an attack from outside your network, these logs can help you identify and troubleshoot those problems.

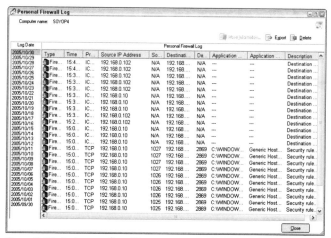

Figure 7-11: Review your firewall logs.

Figure 7-12: The pfirewall.log.

Add Programs to an Exception List

1. Open the control panel for your firewall program.

2. Open the firewall controls. If you see an exception list area, open it. Otherwise, open the personal firewall settings, select your security profile, and click Edit.

3. Open the Exception List tab or controls (see Figure 7-13).

4. Click Add.

5. Type a descriptive name for the exception (see Figure 7-14).

     Although I'm creating a rule for ActiveSync here, you can follow these steps to create an exception for any program that uses network connections. Keep in mind that you may have to create separate rules for outgoing and incoming traffic.

6. Click Browse and locate the program file for the program for which you are creating an exception.

     Program files are usually located in the folder C:\PROGRAM FILES and most have the .EXE file extension.

7. Choose to which target group the exception applies.

8. Choose whether you want the exception rule to allow traffic, deny traffic, or warn you when traffic is about to occur.

     Choose Deny if you want to block a program from using the network.

9. Click OK to save your new exception rule.

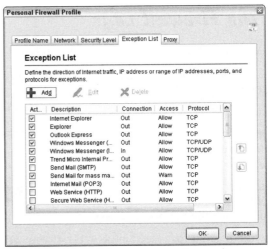

Figure 7-13: Control which programs can use the network.

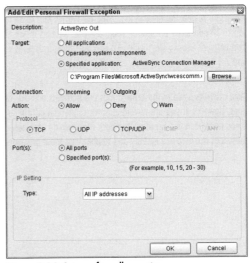

Figure 7-14: Set up a firewall exception.

Block Ping Commands

1. Log in to your router's control panel.

2. Locate the controls for blocking WAN ping commands.

3. Enable WAN ping blocking, as shown in Figure 7-15.

4. Click OK or Apply to save your changes.

 The ping command is used simply to determine if a computer's IP address is valid. Hackers sometimes use the ping command to identify valid, active IP addresses to attack. By blocking ping commands, you make your network less visible to hackers.

The steps here assume that you connect to the Internet using a broadband cable or DSL modem, and that you have a router connecting the broadband modem to the rest of your network. If you connect to the Internet through a dial-up connection, blocking ping commands is less important because your ISP probably gives you a different IP address every time you connect.

Activate the Mac OS X Firewall

1. Choose Apple⇨System Preferences.

2. In System Preferences, click the Sharing icon.

3. In the Sharing window, click Firewall to open the Personal Firewall settings (see Figure 7-16).

4. Click Start to start the firewall.

5. Close the Sharing window.

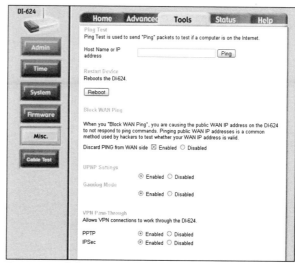

Figure 7-15: Block ping commands from the Internet.

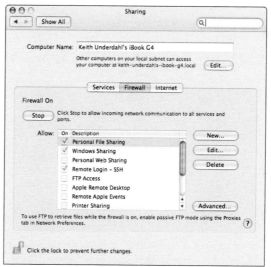

Figure 7-16: Enable the OS X Personal Firewall.

Preventing Unauthorized Network Users

*I*f you live in a neighborhood with lots of other people, sadly, it's probably only a matter of time before unauthorized users start appearing on your network. Even if your neighbors are a long distance away, your network isn't entirely safe.

Of course, we were all taught to share, and many people believe that sharing Internet bandwidth with neighbors is a nice thing to do. However, your Internet service provider may object to the increased traffic, and if one of your neighbors downloads illegal material using your Internet connection, the police will come knocking on your door first.

Before you start viewing your neighbors with suspicion, keep in mind that most wireless network intrusions are inadvertent. Suppose that your next door neighbor buys a Wi-Fi-equipped laptop. He brings it home, fires it up, and discovers that the wireless Internet access works perfectly. He may not realize that he's actually using your Internet connection rather than his own. In this chapter, you discover how to identify unauthorized users on your network, and how to eject them from your network and keep them away.

Review the Access Point Logs

1. Log in to your wireless access point (WAP) using a Web browser. (For just the steps to do so, refer to Chapter 1.)

2. Locate the status or logging area of the access point's control panel. (Most WAP control panels have a Status tab.

3. Click Log to review the access point log (see Figure 8-1).

> If your wireless access point is also a router, you will probably see a lot of router activity listed in the log as well as wireless activity.

4. Note the MAC address shown for each wireless device that has logged in or tried to log in to your WAP.

> In Figure 8-1, the MAC address is listed to the right in the Note column.

5. If the WAP has a status screen dedicated specifically to wireless devices, click the link to open it (see Figure 8-2).

> The Wireless status screen, shown in Figure 8-2, lists wireless devices that are currently connected to your WAP, or were recently connected. If you don't recognize some of the computers in the log, they may be unauthorized users. The log may list additional wireless devices that connected to your WAP earlier, but are no longer connected and thus are not listed in the Wireless status screen.

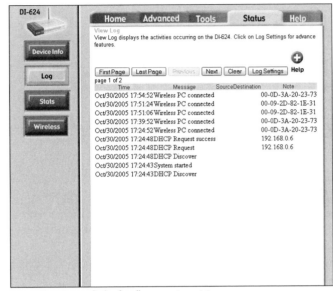

Figure 8-1: Review the log for all access point activity.

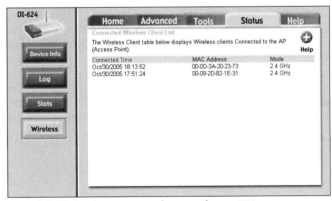

Figure 8-2: Wireless devices are currently connected to your WAP.

Identify Wireless Clients on the Access Point

1. Open a Web browser and log in to the control panel on your WAP.

2. Open the Status tab and go to the Wireless screen (see Figure 8-3).

 The names of the screens for your WAP may be different, but you should have a screen that lists currently connected wireless devices.

3. Note the MAC address for each wireless device connected to your WAP.

4. Open the log for your WAP (see Figure 8-4).

5. Match the MAC addresses from the Wireless status screen with entries in the log.

 By comparing the status screen in Figure 8-3 with the log in Figure 8-4, you can see that one of the wireless devices is a computer named WM_The_Arbiter, which I happen to know is my Wi-Fi-enabled Pocket PC. The other wireless device is an unidentified computer simply named "Wireless PC" in the log. Because I'm unfamiliar with this name, I need to research that device further.

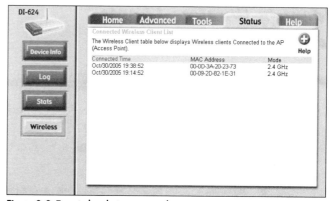

Figure 8-3: Two wireless devices connected.

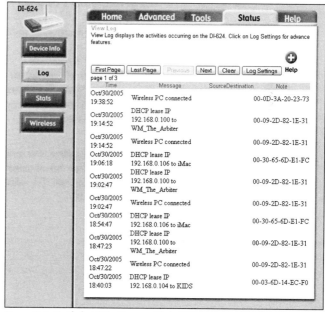

Figure 8-4: Match the MAC addresses with the WAP log.

Identify Wireless Clients with a Security Program

1. Open the control panel for your Internet security program and locate the network security controls (see Figure 8-5).

2. Click the Wi-Fi Detection tool option.

3. In the Wi-Fi Detection screen, click Find to find network computers.

     Most network security programs have a tool to help you detect wireless clients that are connected to your network. The names of buttons and screens may be slightly different in your program, but the function and basic concept should be similar to what is shown here.

4. When the detection process is complete, review the list of computers (see Figure 8-6).

     Keep in mind that although security programs will claim that they are detecting Wi-Fi devices, they're actually detecting all computers on your network. Some of the computers that show up in the list may be connected to your network by Ethernet cables instead of Wi-Fi.

     Some of the listings may be instantly recognizable as other network computers that you own. For example, I know that the computers named KIDS and IMAC are computers that I own. The computer named "WM_THE_ARBITER" is my Pocket PC.

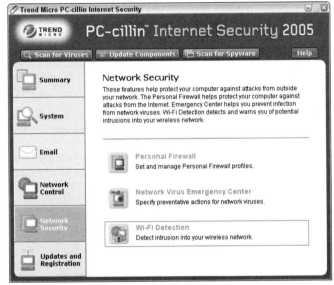

Figure 8-5: The Network Security controls.

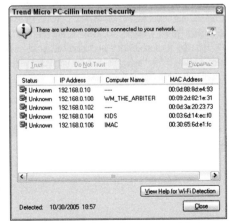

Figure 8-6: Review the list of computers and devices.

5. Click a computer in the list to select it and then click the Properties button.

6. In the resulting dialog box, review details about the device (see Figure 8-7).

Wi-Fi detection utilities usually present several kinds of information which can be used to detect computers, including IP addresses, device types, and in some cases computer names. Keep in mind, however, that the device type detection isn't always totally reliable. For example, on my network an Apple iMac running Mac OS X is detected as a Windows computer, while a Pocket PC — which runs the Windows Mobile operating system — is unknown.

7. Repeat Steps 5 and 6 for each device listed, making note of the MAC addresses listed for any devices that you don't recognize.

8. If a device is positively identified as a computer that you own, select it in the list and click the Trust button. In Figure 8-8, the computer WM_THE_ARBITER is trusted.

Setting a device to Trusted status tells your security program that the device is safe to network with, and you are less likely to have networking problems in the future.

Figure 8-7: View details about each computer.

Figure 8-8: One of my computers is now trusted.

Determine the MAC Address of a Wireless Device

1. On a Windows PC, choose Start⇨Control Panel and then click the Network Connections icon.

2. In the Network Connections window, double-click the network connection currently used to connect to the network and then click the Support tab (see Figure 8-9).

3. Click the Details button and note the Physical Address listed in the Network Connection Details dialog box (see Figure 8-10).

 The Physical Address is actually the MAC address for the network card. MAC stands for *Media Access Control*, and each network card, wireless access point, or wireless card on your network has a unique MAC address.

 If you have a wireless game console adapter, check the label on the underside of the adapter to determine its MAC address. Although game consoles don't normally interact with other computers on your network, they do show up in the router logs as wireless devices, and they have MAC addresses just like any other computer on your network.

 Although MAC addresses are normally a useful way to identify devices on your network, keep in mind that it is possible to spoof a MAC address. In other words, someone could detect a valid MAC address for a device on your network, and then assign that MAC address to a device of their own. They could later use this spoofed MAC address to gain access to your network, without being immediately recognized as an unauthorized intruder.

Figure 8-9: The Support tab for the network connection.

Figure 8-10: The Physical Address is this card's MAC address.

Determine the MAC Address of a Pocket PC

1. Tap the wireless connection icon on the status bar at the top of the Pocket PC's Today screen, and then tap Settings.

2. In the resulting WLAN utility screen, tap the icon for your WLAN connection.

3. Tap the Advanced tab. Note the MAC address (see Figure 8-11).

 The steps here assume you have a Pocket PC running Windows Mobile 5 or better. Most handheld devices with Wi-Fi capability are similar, however.

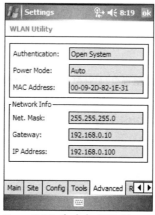

Figure 8-11: Check the MAC address for your Pocket PC.

Determine the MAC Address of a Macintosh PC

1. Choose Apple⇨System Preferences to open System Preferences.

2. Click the Network icon to open the Network control panel.

3. In the Network control panel, note the Ethernet Address (see Figure 8-12). The Ethernet address is the computer's MAC address.

 Make sure that you have the right connection selected in the Show menu of the Network control panel. If you are connecting to the network with an AirPort card, the Built-in Ethernet option won't give you the correct MAC address.

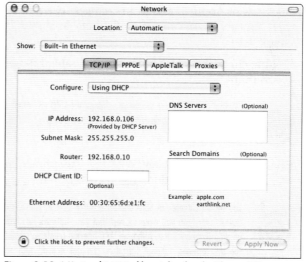

Figure 8-12: A Macintosh's MAC address is listed as the Ethernet Address.

Block a User from the Router

1. Log in to the control panel for your WAP using a Web browser.

2. Locate the filter controls and select MAC filters (see Figure 8-13).

3. Select the Only Deny Computers option to create a MAC filter that will deny access to a specific MAC address.

 See Chapter 6 for steps on MAC address filtering.

4. Enter a name for the rule, and enter the MAC address for the unwanted device.

5. Click OK or Apply to save your changes. The new MAC filter appears in your list of MAC filters, as shown in Figure 8-14.

6. Double-check that SSID broadcast is disabled in your access point.

 Disable SSID broadcast *before* you change the SSID and other network security keys as described in the following step.

7. Change the SSID, WEP key, WPA-PSK passphrase, and administrator password for your access point.

 You should change the SSID and all security keys in your wireless devices any time you even *suspect* that your network has had an unauthorized intrusion. Although MAC filtering creates a roadblock for the intruder, diligent intruders can get around that roadblock either by MAC address spoofing, or by simply using a different computer.

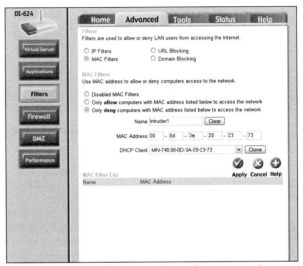

Figure 8-13: Filter unauthorized MAC addresses from your network.

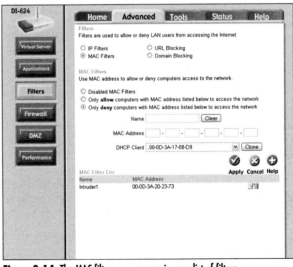

Figure 8-14: The MAC filter now appears in your list of filters.

Block a User with a Security Program

1. Open your Internet security program, open the Wi-Fi detection screen used for detecting computers on your network, and find local computers, as I describe earlier in this chapter.

2. Select the computer you want to restrict and click Properties.

3. Block access from the offending computer. In Trend Micro's Internet security program, shown in Figure 8-15, click the Add Exception button to block the computer.

 Blocking an intruder using an Internet security program installed on a specific computer does protect the data on your computer, but it does not block the intruder from the rest of your network.

Figure 8-15: Click Add Exception to block out this computer.

Part III
Improving Your Network's Performance

The 5th Wave   By Rich Tennant

"The kids are getting up right now.
When we wired the house we added
vibrating pager technology to their
bunkbeds."

Monitoring Network Performance

*I*f you want to keep your wireless network running fast and efficient, you need to continuously monitor its performance. The speed of a Wi-Fi network is measured in megabits per second, or Mbps. Ideally, your Wi-Fi gear should be running at 54 Mbps — the speed of 802.11g Wi-Fi gear — or better. However, some components may cause your network to slow down to 802.11b speed, which is 11 Mbps. At this slower speed, transferring files takes longer, multimedia plays poorly, and downloading e-mail and Web pages takes longer.

In this chapter, you find out how to measure the speed and range of your Wi-Fi network, and how to determine the IP address of each computer on your network. Knowing each computer's IP address helps you troubleshoot various network problems and identify potential bottlenecks.

Most manufacturers of Wi-Fi gear now offer special speed boosting technologies designed to let you network at speeds even faster than 54 Mbps. Keep in mind, however, that these speed-boosting technologies are usually proprietary. Therefore, to take advantage of the faster speeds all of your networking gear has to be from the same manufacturer. A 102 Mbps Wi-Fi card from Manufacturer A probably won't work at 102 Mbps if it's connecting to a 102 Mbps access point from Manufacturer B.

Chapter 9

Get ready to . . .

Review Wireless Bandwidth Statistics

1. Log in to your access point using a Web browser.

2. Locate the traffic statistics screen in the access point's control panel. Look for a Traffic or Stats button or link (see Figure 9-1).

3. Review statistics for the wireless portion of your network and compare it to other network traffic.

 WAN stands for *wide area network*, and LAN stands for *local area network*. The WAN is usually your Internet connection, and the LAN is your local network. LAN traffic includes wireless traffic, so if you don't have any Ethernet wired computers the LAN and wireless statistics should be about the same.

 Reset the counters and then check them 24 hours later. Do this on a regular basis to get an idea of your normal daily bandwidth. An abnormal surge in wireless traffic may indicate that an unauthorized user is on your network.

4. Locate the list of wireless clients and make sure that each device belongs to you (see Figure 9-2).

 I discuss how to identify wireless users in Chapter 8. Even if all of the devices belong to you, disabling unused wireless devices (such as game consoles or printers that are not currently in use) can help speed up your network.

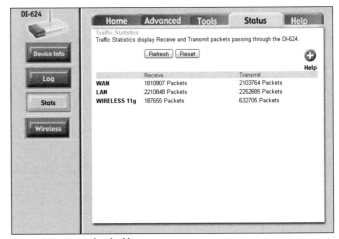

Figure 9-1: Monitor bandwidth.

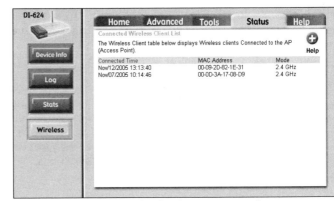

Figure 9-2: Check the number of wireless clients on your network.

Receive Router Logs by E-Mail

1. Log in to the router's control panel using a Web browser.

2. Open the Logs screen of the router control panel and click the Log Settings button or link.

3. In the log settings, select the type of information you want e-mailed to you (see Figure 9-3).

 System activity includes DHCP requests, which occur when a computer joins your network.

4. Enter the SMTP Server for outgoing mail and your e-mail address and click OK or Apply.

 You can obtain the address for your SMTP mail server from your ISP. SMTP servers are used for outgoing mail.

Identify Computers on Your Network

1. Log in to the router's control panel using a Web browser.

2. Open the DHCP screen in the router control panel and locate the list of DHCP clients (see Figure 9-4).

3. Note how many computers are using your network.

 Each computer on your network must have a unique IP address, which is assigned by the router's DHCP server. The DHCP client list lists computers currently or recently active on your network.

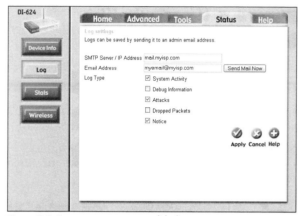

Figure 9-3: Set up your router to e-mail the logs to you.

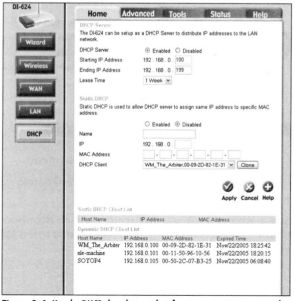

Figure 9-4: Use the DHCP client lists to identify computers on your network.

Determine a Windows PC's IP Address

1. Choose Start⇨All Programs⇨Accessories⇨ Communication⇨Network Connections.

2. In the resulting Network Connections window, click your current network connection once to select it.

3. Note the IP address and other information under Details on the left side of the Network Connections window (see Figure 9-5).

 You can use the Network Connections window to check the IP address of any Windows network adapter, whether it is a wireless adapter (such as the one shown in Figure 9-5), or an Ethernet adapter.

 If you have an older version of Windows, open the MS-DOS Command Prompt from the Windows Start menu. At the command prompt, type IPCONFIG and press Enter. The computer's IP address and other network information will be listed in the Command Prompt window.

Determine a Mac's IP Address

1. Open System Preferences from the Apple menu.

2. Click the Network icon in the System Preferences window.

3. Select your current network connection in the Show menu, and then note the IP address that is listed (see Figure 9-6).

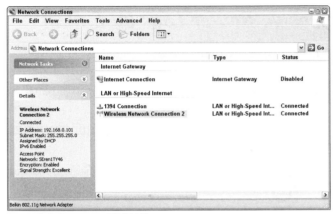

Figure 9-5: Determine a PC's IP Address.

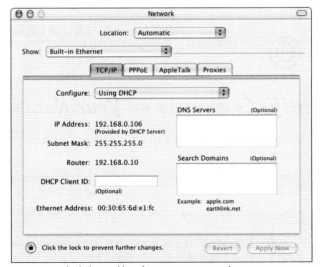

Figure 9-6: Check the IP address for your current network connection.

Determine a Pocket PC's IP Address

1. Tap the Wi-Fi connection icon on the Pocket PC's Today screen.

2. In the wireless LAN utility, tap the Advanced tab (see Figure 9-7).

3. Note the IP address listed on the Advanced tab.

 If your Pocket PC was connected to a desktop computer using ActiveSync, it may have obtained an IP address from the desktop PC instead of the router. The steps here assume that your Pocket PC is connected through Wi-Fi to your wireless router/WAP.

Check the Speed of a Wireless PC

1. Double-click the system tray icon for your wireless connection.

 Remember that the Windows system tray is the area in the lower-right corner next to the clock. If you don't have a system tray icon for your wireless connection, choose Start⇨All Programs⇨Accessories⇨ Communications⇨Network Connections and then double-click the listing for your wireless network connection.

2. Note the speed shown for the connection (see Figure 9-8).

 Most wireless connection management utilities have a speed measurement similar to the one shown here. Simply open the connection's status window to review a current graph of connection speed.

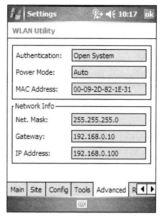

Figure 9-7: Note the Pocket PC's IP address.

Figure 9-8: Check the speed of your connection.

Measure Your Wi-Fi Range

1. Open the status window for your wireless connection. (If you're using a Pocket PC, open the Config tab of the wireless LAN utility, as shown in Figure 9-9.)

2. Move the computer to different locations and note the signal strength.

3. Note the signal strength in different locations. In Windows, right-click the wireless connection icon in the system tray to see the Wi-Fi signal strength (see Figure 9-10).

 Geographic distance isn't the only factor that affects the range of your Wi-Fi network. Brick walls, heavy furniture, and other objects can create additional interference. Just because the signal strength is poor in your living room doesn't mean that a neighbor two houses away can't receive your network's signal.

 Some Wi-Fi antennas are stronger than others. If you have more than one wireless computer, test your Wi-Fi range using every device, noting which unit seems to get the best reception. Use the unit with the best reception to test the range of your network.

Figure 9-9: A poor Wi-Fi signal.

Figure 9-10: An excellent connection.

Improving the Speed and Range of Your Network

Wireless networks make it easier to use technology throughout your home or small office. However, you may find that your wireless network doesn't perform quite as well as you'd hoped. Performance problems with wireless networks can usually be divided into two categories:

➡ **Speed:** Sometimes your wireless network may seem to operate very slowly. You're not likely to notice slow Wi-Fi speeds when browsing the Internet wirelessly, but you may notice it if you are copying large files over Wi-Fi or trying to stream high-quality audio and video. You may be able speed up your network by identifying speed bottlenecks and removing slow devices from the network.

➡ **Range:** Wi-Fi range is unpredictable. If you want to increase the range of your wireless network, you can do a number of things. Some things — like range-extending antennas and Wi-Fi repeaters — cost money, while others don't.

This chapter helps you improve the speed and range of your wireless network by avoiding interference, using high-gain antennas, and using special devices designed specifically to boost Wi-Fi range.

Identify Wi-Fi Bottlenecks

1. Check the documentation or labeling for wireless devices to make sure that they are compatible with the 802.11g Wi-Fi standard.

2. Open wireless networking utilities on suspect devices and check the transmission rate (see Figure 10-1).

 In Figure 10-1, the Tx Rate is 11Mbps, which is the speed of 802.11b network gear. If this device is only compatible with 802.11b, installing it could cause your entire network to slow down to 802.11b speeds.

3. Disable 802.11b gear when maximum Wi-Fi speed is needed.

Adjust Access Point Speed Settings

1. Log in to your access point using a Web browser. (For just the steps to do so, refer to Chapter 1.)

2. Locate the performance controls (see Figure 10-2).

3. Select the Enabled radio button by the 802.11g Only Mode option and click OK or Apply.

 Adjusting this setting forces your wireless network to perform at the faster 802.11g speed, but 802.11b gear may be unable to access the network.

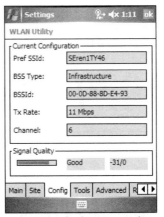

Figure 10-1: This device is networking at 802.11b speeds.

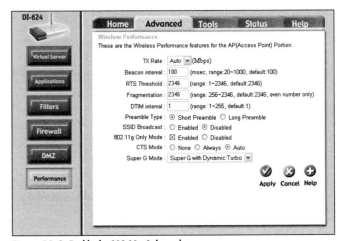

Figure 10-2: Enable the 802.11g Only mode.

Network Faster than the Speed of G

1. Purchase an access point and wireless adapters that use the same wireless acceleration technology.

    Belkin, D-Link, Linksys, Netgear, and most other manufacturers of Wi-Fi gear offer accelerator technology that allows connections even faster than 802.11g gear. However, these accelerator technologies are usually proprietary, which means that to actually use the higher speeds the access point and all Wi-Fi adapters must be of the same brand and have the same accelerator technology.

2. Log in to the access point's control panel and enable the accelerator technology (see Figure 10-3).

    Acceleration controls are usually found on the Wireless, Advanced, or Performance screens. Keep in mind that some accelerator technologies may be incompatible with networking gear from other manufacturers. If some of your devices are unable to access the network after you turn on acceleration features, you may need to disable the acceleration.

3. Launch the wireless adapter software on the client computer (see Figure 10-4).

    It is usually necessary to use the adapter's proprietary software to take advantage of accleration technology. The Windows wireless connection manager can only manage 802.11a/b/g networks.

4. Make sure that the client software uses the same acceleration settings as the access point.

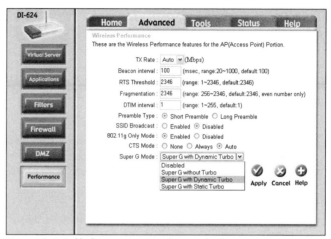

Figure 10-3: Enable the access point's accelerator technology.

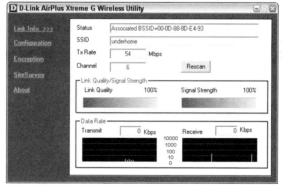

Figure 10-4: The wireless adapter's utility program.

Position the Access Point for Best Range

1. Choose a location that is central to your wireless clients, as shown in Figure 10-5.

2. Mount the access point high and away from obstructions.

 Try to mount the access point away from heavy furniture and other large obstacles. Avoid placing the access points near brick, cement, or plaster walls. Windows, mirrors, and other reflective surfaces can also reduce signal range.

 Experiment with different locations to see which gives the best range.

Eliminate Wi-Fi Interference

1. Do not position the access point near appliances that cause interference on the 2.4 GHz band (see Figure 10-6).

 Microwaves and baby monitors often cause interference on the 2.4 GHz band.

2. Try to use cordless phones that use the 900 MHz or 5.8 GHz bands.

 In the unlikely event that you have an 802.11a network, you may want to avoid 5.8 GHz phones because 802.11a gear uses the 5 GHz band.

3. Separate Bluetooth and Wi-Fi gear, if possible. Bluetooth signals can cause minor inference with 802.11b/g gear.

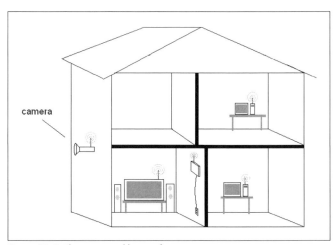

Figure 10-5: Choose a central location for your access point.

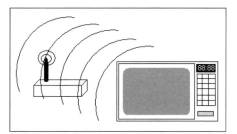

Figure 10-6: Microwave ovens cause Wi-Fi interference.

Add a Range Extending Antenna to Your Access Point

1. Choose a directional or omni-directional antenna (see Figure 10-7).

 Directional antennas like the one on the left can be aimed to concentrate the range in a specific direction. Omni-directional antennas like the one on the right increase range in any direction.

2. Connect the antenna to your access point.

3. If you have a directional antenna, point it in the direction where you want to most boost your Wi-Fi range.

Use a High Gain Antenna with a Wi-Fi Adapter

1. Obtain an antenna that is compatible with your Wi-Fi adapter.

2. Connect the high gain antenna to the adapter.

3. Position the antenna as high as possible for best reception (see Figure 10-8).

 Generally speaking, you can only add a high gain antenna to a Wi-Fi adapter if the adapter has a removable antenna. USB and cardbus adapters usually do not have removable antennas, but PCI card Wi-Fi adapters usually do have removable antennas.

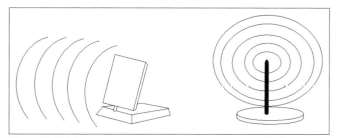

Figure 10-7: A directional antenna lets you increase range in a specific direction.

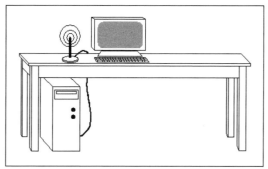

Figure 10-8: Place the Wi-Fi client antenna on top of your desk.

Increase Range with a Wi-Fi Repeater

1. Obtain a Wi-Fi repeater or range extender.

2. Use an Ethernet cable to connect the repeater to your router/access point, or directly to a computer.

3. Log in to the repeater's control panel using a Web browser, just as you would log in to your regular access point.

4. Configure the repeater to use the same SSID and encryption settings as your regular access point.

5. After configuration is complete, disconnect the Ethernet cable and position the repeater about halfway between the access point and the most distant computer, as shown in Figure 10-9.

 When positioning a repeater, it must be within range of your regular access point.

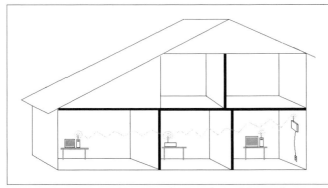

Figure 10-9: A range extender increases the range of your Wi-Fi network.

Troubleshooting Network Problems

Chapter

11

*W*ireless networking is only cool and convenient when it works right. Networking problems can — and probably will — occur at some point. You've probably been there before; you try to log on and you can't download e-mail, print a picture, or copy files over the network.

The causes of networking problems are many and varied, but they can usually be solved by following a methodical troubleshooting process. In this chapter, I take you through the troubleshooting process in order from the simplest solutions to the more complex:

➡ **Restart:** When you contact a software company for technical support, often the first thing they tell you to do is restart your computer. You do this first because it's easy, and (more often than not) it works. Network problems are also sometimes solved by restarting a connection or the router.

➡ **Update:** Computer software is ever changing. An update of Windows or the Macintosh OS may also require you to update other programs. I show you which updates often solve networking problems and how to perform those updates.

➡ **Identify:** If restarting and updating don't solve the problem, then you need to identify the source of the problem. Is a defective access point the culprit, or is the problem on one of your computers?

Get ready to . . .

Refresh a PC's Wireless Connection

1. Double-click the system tray icon for the computer's wireless connection manager utility to open it.

2. In the resulting dialog box, click the Repair button (see Figure 11-1) to disable the wireless connection.

 If you use the Windows wireless connection manager, simply right-click the wireless connection icon in the system tray (the area in the lower-right corner next to the clock) and choose Repair. Windows will automatically disable and then reconnect the wireless connection.

 If refreshing the wireless connection does not restore your wireless connectivity, try restarting the computer. If that does not work, your next step is to restart DHCP or reboot the access point as described later in this chapter.

Refresh a Pocket PC's Wireless Connection

1. Tap the Wi-Fi icon in the lower-right corner of the Today screen to open the WLAN utility.

2. Tap Turn Off (see Figure 11-2).

3. Wait about five seconds and then tap Turn On to reactivate the wireless connection.

 Generally speaking, if your wireless connection icon shows green it is not necessary to refresh the connection. Green suggests an active and successful wireless connection, and that your connectivity problem is caused by something else.

Figure 11-1: Refresh the wireless connection.

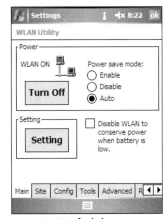

Figure 11-2: Refresh the connection on a Pocket PC.

Restart DHCP Service

1. Log in to your router or wireless access point (WAP) using a Web browser (see Chapter 1).

2. Click the DHCP button or tab (depending on your router) to open the DHCP server controls.

 DHCP stands for *Dynamic Host Control Protocol,* and is what assigns unique IP addresses to every computer on the network. Restarting DHCP can help resolve IP conflicts or other DHCP problems.

3. Select the Disabled radio button for the DHCP server, and then click OK or Apply to turn off the DHCP server (see Figure 11-3).

4. Return to the DHCP controls, choose the Enabled radio button, and click OK or Apply again to re-activate DHCP.

 You may need to reboot other computers on your network to complete the re-assigning of IP addresses.

Reboot the Access Point

1. Log in to your router/WAP using a Web browser (described in Chapter 1).

2. Locate the control for rebooting the WAP, as shown in Figure 11-4, and click it to reboot the WAP.

 If you are unable to locate a control for rebooting the WAP, simply unplug the WAP's power cord, wait about five seconds, and then plug the power back in.

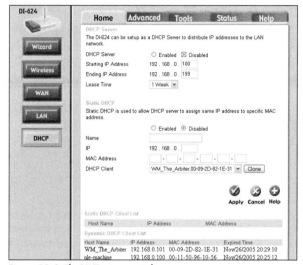

Figure 11-3: The DHCP server controls.

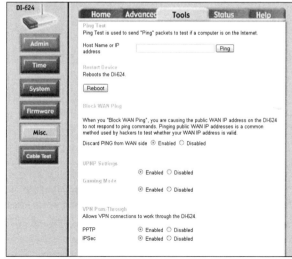

Figure 11-4: Reboot the WAP.

Troubleshoot a Bad Wireless Connection

1. Refresh the wireless connection that is giving you trouble, as I describe earlier in this chapter.

    These steps help you troubleshoot a bad connection. Stop following the steps when the connection problem is solved.

2. Temporarily disable the firewall or Internet security software on the computer that is having connection troubles (see Chapter 7).

3. Open the wireless connection manager and make sure that the SSID is correct. Also make sure that encryption settings and keys match the settings in your WAP.

4. Restart DHCP on your WAP; if necessary reboot the WAP.

5. If the troublesome Wi-Fi adapter is removable — such as a USB, cardbus, or Ethernet bridge adapter — remove or disconnect it and disconnect any power cords. Then reconnect the device.

6. Right-click the My Computer icon in the Windows Start menu and choose Properties.

7. In the System Properties dialog box, click the Hardware tab and then click the Device Manager button (see Figure 11-5).

8. In the Device Manager window, click the plus-sign next to Network Adapters (see Figure 11-6).

    If you see a yellow exclamation mark next to the name of the adapter, something is wrong. Right-click it and choose Uninstall, restart Windows, and then re-install the driver software as described in the manufacturer's instructions.

Figure 11-5: The System Properties dialog box.

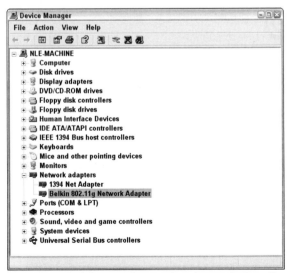

Figure 11-6: Check the status of your wireless adapter in the Device Manager.

Update the Access Point's Firmware

1. Log in to your router or WAP using a Web browser (refer to Chapter 1).

 Always perform firmware updates using a wired Ethernet connection to the router/WAP. Upgrading firmware over a Wi-Fi connection may cause damage to the WAP.

2. Find the screen that allows you to back up your router or WAP settings (see Figure 11-7).

3. Click Save and then save the settings file to a hard drive on your computer.

 Saving your router/WAP settings will make it easier to recover if a problem occurs during the update.

4. Find the screen that helps you update your firmware (see Figure 11-8).

5. Right-click the link to check for updates and choose the Open in New Window option to open the link in a new browser window.

6. Follow the instructions to download the firmware update.

7. After the update file is downloaded, click the Browse button to locate the update and then click OK or Apply to install it.

8. Return to the screen for loading settings and reload your settings.

 Usually, when you update firmware the SSID, encryption, and other security settings are restored to factory defaults.

 Firmware updates may add features, fix problems, or add support for new technologies that weren't available when the router/WAP was first produced. For example, I had to update the firmware in my WAP to use the Xbox Live service.

Figure 11-7: Back up your settings.

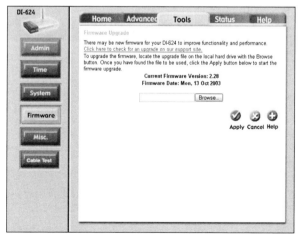

Figure 11-8: Check for and install firmware updates.

Update Driver Software for Wireless Devices

1. Right-click the My Computer icon in the Windows Start menu and choose Properties.

2. In the System Properties dialog box, click the Hardware tab and then click the Device Manager button.

3. In the Device Manager window, click the plus-sign next to Network Adapters to expand the list of adapters.

4. Right-click the network adapter you want to update and choose Update Driver from the menu that appears.

5. In the Hardware Update Wizard, choose whether or not you want to connect to Windows Update to check for an update, as shown in Figure 11-9, and then click Next.

6. If you already downloaded an updated driver from the manufacturer's Web site, select the Install From a List or Specific Location option. Otherwise, choose the first option. Click Next.

 If you chose the first option, Windows Update will check for and automatically install an update, if one is found. In this case, no further steps are necessary.

7. If you are installing from a specific location, choose the Don't Search option in the following dialog box and click Next.

8. Choose the appropriate driver as shown in Figure 11-10, or click the Have Disk button and browse to the location containing the updated driver.

Figure 11-9: Check for an update.

Figure 11-10: Choose your driver or browse.

Ping a Network Computer

1. Determine the IP address of the computer you want to ping.

 In Chapter 9, I go over how to determine a computer's IP address. You can also ping your router/WAP, which usually has the IP address 192.168.0.1.

2. In Windows choose Start⇨All Programs⇨Accessories⇨ Command Prompt.

3. At the command prompt, type (see Figure 11-11):

```
ping 192.168.0.1
```

 Replace the IP address above (192.168.0.1) with the address you want to ping. A successful ping results in four replies.

4. Type Exit at the command prompt and press Enter to close the Command Prompt window.

5. Repeat the ping process from other computers. You can also ping from a computer other than a Windows PC:

- **Pocket PC:** Tap Start⇨Settings, tap the Connections tab, and then tap the WLAN Utility icon. Tap Settings and open the Tools tab. Type the IP address you want to ping and tap Start. Figure 11-12 shows a successful ping.

- **Mac:** Open the Applications folder on your hard drive, and then open the Utilities sub folder. Double-click the Network Utility and click the Ping tab to bring it to the front. Type the IP address address you want to ping in the space provided and click Ping.

Figure 11-11: Use the command prompt to ping network computers.

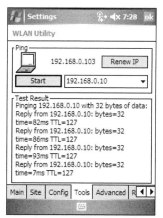

Figure 11-12: Ping from a Pocket PC.

Troubleshoot Network Access Problems

1. Temporarily disable the firewall or Internet security software on the computer that is having connection troubles.

    These steps help you troubleshoot a bad network connection. Stop following the steps when the problem is solved.

2. Ping the router from the computer that is giving trouble, and also try to ping another computer on the network. Likewise, ping the troublesome computer from another computer on the network.

    A ping test tells you if the computers are able to connect to each other on the most basic level over the network.

3. Make sure that the computer is set to automatically obtain an IP address from the DHCP server in your router/WAP.

4. Restart DHCP on your WAP, and then if necessary reboot the WAP.

5. Make sure each computer on the network has the same workgroup name. In Windows, right-click My Computer and choose Properties.

6. In the resulting System Properties dialog box, click the Computer Name tab (see Figure 11-13). Each computer on the network should have the same workgroup name.

7. Update the driver software for the offending network adapter.

Figure 11-13: The System Properties dialog box, Computer Name tab.

 I show how to set up computers as DHCP clients in Chapter 2.

Part IV
Using Someone Else's Network

The 5th Wave   By Rich Tennant

"Ironically, he went out there looking for a 'hot spot.'"

Finding and Using Public Hotspots

M ost of this book is about home networking. Wireless networking technologies make home networks a lot more fun and easy to use, but you don't have to leave Wi-Fi behind when you leave home. Hotspots are another popular way to use wireless networking. Hotspots are open networks that hotels, coffee shops, libraries, universities, airports, and other establishments make available for anyone with a Wi-Fi-equipped portable computer. When you connect to a hotspot, you can browse the Internet, check e-mail, or perform other online tasks. Hotspots generally fall into two categories:

➡ **Free:** You may not be able to get a free lunch, but you can take advantage of lots of free hotspots. Free hotspots are usually found at public institutions or at businesses (such as hotels) where Internet access is considered an incidental perk.

➡ **Subscription:** Most hotspots require a service fee or subscription to an access service. Companies such as T-Mobile and iPass run nationwide hotspot networks that you can access when you pay a single monthly subscription fee.

In this chapter, I go over how to find and use hotspots, as well as how to disconnect from hotspots when you are no longer using them.

Chapter
12

Get ready to . . .

Protect Your Files from Network Access

1. Choose Start➪Control Panel and then click the Windows Firewall icon.

    If your Windows Control Panel is set to Category view, click the Security Center icon and then click Windows Firewall.

2. Make sure that the Windows Firewall is turned on and then click the Exceptions tab (see Figure 12-1).

3. Click the box next to File and Printer Sharing to deselect the option and click OK.

    Blocking File and Printer Sharing prevent other network users from accessing files on your computer.

4. In the Windows Control Panel, click the Network Connections icon.

5. Right-click the network connection you use to connect to the company network and choose Properties.

6. In the Network Connection Properties dialog box, deselect the File and Printer Sharing for Microsoft Networks option (see Figure 12-2).

7. Click OK to close the Network Connection Properties dialog box.

    Follow these steps again to reactivate file sharing later when you are disconnected from the corporate network.

Figure 12-1: Windows Firewall dialog box, Exceptions tab.

Figure 12-2: Disable File and Printer Sharing.

Find Hotspots

1. Visit a Wi-Fi hotspot locator Web site.

 JiWire.com is one of several hotspot locator Web sites available on the Internet. To find others, search for "Wi-Fi hotspots" on any major Internet search engine.

2. Search for hotspots using your address, city, or postal code, as shown in Figure 12-3.

 Most hotspot locators let you refine your search to a specific range. You can also usually specify whether you want to find free or pay hotspots.

3. Check additional local resources including:

- Local schools and city governments sometimes offer wireless Internet access. In Figure 12-4, the Web site of the City of Lebanon, Oregon provides details on a local free and low-cost wireless network.

- Local businesses may offer hotspots. Some promote their hotspots vigorously, and some don't.

- Subscribe to a national hotspot network service provider, such as iPass or T-Mobile. If you subscribe to T-Mobile's hotspot service, for example, you can access hotspots in Starbucks, Borders, Kinkos, and many other popular businesses.

Figure 12-3: JiWire.com is an excellent online hotspot locator.

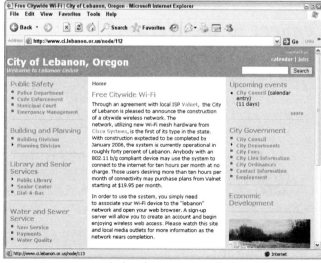

Figure 12-4: Businesses, schools, and cities sometimes offer free Wi-Fi.

Search for a Wi-Fi Signal

1. Launch your wireless connection utility.

    You can usually launch your connection utility by double-clicking your wireless connection icon in the Windows system tray (the area in the lower-right corner of the screen next to the clock).

2. Open the list of available wireless networks, as shown in Figure 12-5.

    If you let Windows manage your wireless connections, right-click the wireless connection icon in the system tray and choose View Available Wireless Networks.

3. If the wireless network you want to use doesn't appear in the list, click the Refresh button.

Connect to the Network

1. Open the list of available wireless networks in your connection utility.

2. Select the network to which you want to connect, as shown in Figure 12-6, and click Connect or Configure (depending on your connection utility).

    You may need to follow additional steps to join the network, particularly if the network requires a subscription. Usually, once you purchase a subscription you can log in to the network through a Web browser.

Figure 12-5: View the list of available networks.

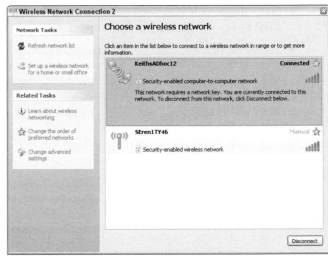

Figure 12-6: Choose a network to which you want to connect.

Monitor the Connection

1. Double-click the wireless connection icon in the Windows system tray.

2. If Windows manages your wireless connection, check the link status on the General tab (see Figure 12-7).

   > If you use a different program to manage your wireless connection, find the tab or screen which shows the status of your wireless link.

3. Make a note of the speed and signal strength.

   > If the quality of the connection is poor, try moving your computer to a different location so that it is closer to the wireless access point and out of the way of furniture and other large obstructions.

   > If the hotspot is an 802.11b network, the maximum connection speed will be 11.0 Mbps, even if your 802.11g wireless adapter is theoretically capable of faster speeds.

4. Check the bandwidth statistics for the connection (see Figure 12-8).

   > Bandwidth is usually listed by number of packets sent and received. Monitoring the bandwidth is a good idea so that you know your typical usage level. If you observe an unusually high bandwidth, it is possible that an unauthorized user is accessing your computer.

Figure 12-7: Monitor the quality of the network connection.

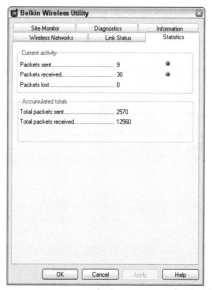

Figure 12-8: Keep track of your connection bandwidth.

Disable Automatic Connection

1. Open the wireless connection utility for your wireless adapter.

2. Locate the setting that controls whether or not you want to automatically connect to non-preferred networks.

    If you use Windows to manage your connection, go to the Wireless Networks tab of the Wireless Network Connection Properties dialog box and click Advanced to open the Advanced dialog box.

3. Select the Automatically Connect to Non-Preferred Networks checkbox and then click Close (see Figure 12-9).

4. Select a preferred network in the network list, and then click Properties.

5. Clear the setting to automatically connect to the network when it is in range. When using the Windows connection manager, click the Connection tab and then deselect the Connect When this Network is in Range checkbox, as shown in Figure 12-10.

6. Click OK to close all dialog boxes and save your settings.

    Disabling automatic connection is a good idea particularly if you pay by the hour for network access.

Figure 12-9: Don't let your computer automatically connect to non-preferred networks.

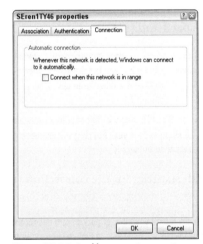

Figure 12-10: Disable automatic connection for preferred networks.

Protect Your Computer from Public Access

1. Exercise good physical security practices by typing passwords in privacy, and by not leaving your laptop unattended.

2. Disable file sharing as described earlier in this chapter.

3. Install and use antivirus and firewall programs, such as the one shown in Figure 12-11.

> If you don't have another firewall program, at least use the Windows Firewall that is built in to Windows XP SP2 and later. However, I recommend that you upgrade to a more powerful third-party firewall program, available from any computer retailer.

4. Disable automatic network connection, as I describe earlier in this chapter.

> If you leave automatic network connection enabled, your computer may connect to rogue wireless access points that mimic the hotspot to steal your passwords and other sensitive information.

5. Check the SSID of the network you are joining, as shown in Figure 12-12, and only connect to networks with a known and trusted SSID.

> The owner of the hotspot should provide you with the proper SSID. If you don't recognize a network's SSID, don't connect to it.

6. Disable your wireless radio when you are done using the wireless network. I describe how to disconnect in the following task.

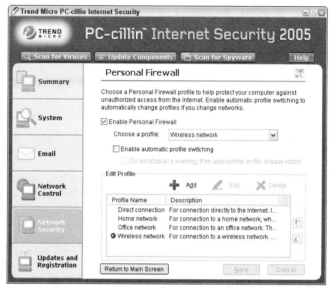

Figure 12-11: Protect your computer with a firewall program.

Figure 12-12: Don't connect to unknown and untrusted networks.

Leave the Public Network

1. When you are done using the wireless network, turn off your wireless radio.

   • If you use Windows to manage your wireless connection, simply right-click the wireless connection icon in the Windows system tray and choose Disable.

   • If you use another wireless connection manager, open it and turn off the wireless radio (see Figure 12-13).

    Turning off the radio protects your computer from unauthorized access, and it prevents you from racking up hourly access charges when you aren't actually using the network.

2. If you don't plan to use a wireless network again in the future, select it in your list of preferred networks and click Remove or Delete.

    If you connect to your company's network using Ethernet, you may want to disable the Wi-Fi adapter in your laptop while you're at work so that other wireless devices in your office don't accidentally connect to your computer. Right-click the wireless connection icon in the Windows system tray (the area in the lower-right corner next to the clock) and choose Disable from the menu that appears. You can re-activate the wireless connection later using the Network Connections icon in the Windows Control Panel.

Figure 12-13: Disable your wireless radio when you're done using the network.

Making Ad Hoc Peer-to-Peer Wireless Connections

Chapter 13

Most of the tasks in this book show you how to create and use wireless networks using the *infrastructure* network model. In an infrastructure network, wireless devices communicate with each other through a wireless access point (WAP). An infrastructure network is much like a wired Ethernet network, but without the wires.

You can also network wirelessly without a router or WAP. Wireless computers can connect directly to each other to create an *ad hoc* network. Ad hoc networks are useful when:

➠ You want to quickly copy files between two wireless computers, and no WAP is currently available.

➠ You only have two computers, and you don't want to spend the extra money on a router/WAP.

 If you set up your home network as an ad hoc network, set up Internet Connection Sharing (see Chapter 2) on the computer that connects to the Internet. Doing so allows you to share your Internet connection over your ad hoc network.

➠ You want to create a temporary network between two Wi-Fi-equipped game consoles for system-link gaming.

This chapter describes how to quickly set up and use ad hoc networks.

Enable Ad Hoc Networking

1. Choose Start⇨My Network Places and then click View Network Connections under Network Tasks on the left side of the screen.

2. Right-click the Wireless Network Adapter icon and choose Properties.

3. In the Wireless Network Connection Properties dialog box, click the Wireless Networks tab and then click Add.

4. On the Association tab of the Wireless Network Properties dialog box, enter a network name (SSID) for the ad hoc network, as shown in Figure 13-1.

5. Enable WEP encryption, deselect The Key is Provided for Me Automatically check box, and enter a WEP key in the two spaces provided.

 SSIDs and WEP keys are explained in Chapter 6. Your WEP key should be 10 or 26 characters long and use a combination of the numbers 0–9 and the letters A–F.

6. Select the This is a Computer-to-Computer (Ad Hoc) Network check box.

7. Click OK. The ad hoc network now appears under Preferred networks, as shown in Figure 13-2.

8. Click OK to close the Wireless Network Connection Properties dialog box.

 Repeat these steps on each computer to create the ad hoc connection.

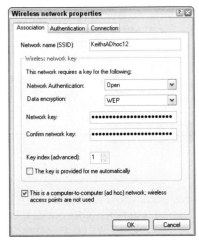

Figure 13-1: Create a SSID and WEP key for your ad hoc network.

Figure 13-2: The ad hoc network is now a preferred network.

Set Up Ad Hoc Networking on a Pocket PC

1. Tap the Wi-Fi icon in the lower-right corner of the Today screen to open the WLAN settings.

   Alternatively, tap Start⇨Settings, tap the Connections tab, and then tap the WLAN Utility icon.

2. Tap Setting.

3. In the list of wireless networks, tap Add New.

4. On the General tab that appears, enter the SSID for your ad hoc network next to Network Name and select the This is a Device-to-Device (Ad Hoc) Connection option.

5. Tap the Network Key tab (see Figure 13-3).

6. Choose WEP for the encryption type, and enter the Network key.

   SSIDs and WEP keys are explained in Chapter 6. Your WEP key should be 10 or 26 characters long and use a combination of the numbers 0–9 and the letters A–F.

7. Tap OK to see the ad hoc network listed (see Figure 13-4).

Figure 13-3: The Network Key tab.

Figure 13-4: The ad hoc network is ready to use.

Connect to the Ad Hoc Network

1. Choose Start⇨My Network Places.

2. In the My Network Places window, click View Network Connections under Network Tasks on the left side of the screen.

3. Double-click the Wireless Connection icon to open the Wireless Network Connection Status dialog box.

4. Click View Wireless Networks.

5. If you are currently connected to another network — such as a WAP-based infrastructure network — select it in the list of networks, and then click the Disconnect button.

6. Select the ad hoc network and click Connect. The connection acquires a network address and then connects, as shown in Figure 13-5.

 If the ad hoc network doesn't appear in your list of available networks, click Change Advanced Settings under Related Tasks on the left side of the screen. This should reveal any ad hoc networks that you have configured on the computer.

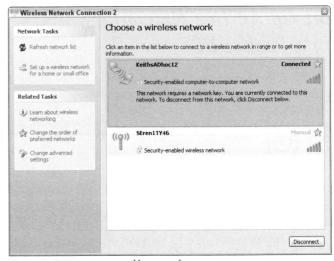

Figure 13-5: Connect to your ad hoc network.

Connect a Pocket PC to an Ad Hoc Network

1. Tap the Wi-Fi icon in the lower-right corner of the Today screen.

2. In the WLAN utility, tap Setting.

3. Tap-and-hold on the ad hoc network and then choose Connect from the menu that appears, as shown in Figure 13-6.

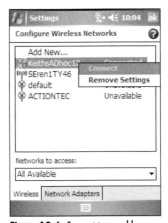

Figure 13-6: Connect to an ad hoc network from a Pocket PC.

Disable Infrastructure Networking

1. Double-click the Wireless Connection icon in the Windows system tray.

     The system tray is the area in the lower-right corner next to the clock.

2. In the resulting Wireless Network Connection Status dialog box, click Properties.

3. In the Wireless Network Connection Properties dialog box, click the Wireless Networks tab and then click the Advanced button.

4. In the Advanced dialog box shown in Figure 13-7, select the Computer-to-Computer (Ad Hoc) Networks Only option and click the Close button.

5. In the Wireless Network Connection Properties dialog box, make sure that only ad hoc networks are listed (see Figure 13-8).

6. Click OK and then click the Close button to close all open dialog boxes.

     Choosing ad hoc networks prevents your computer from automatically connecting to available infrastructure networks, thereby simplifying the process of making ad hoc connections.

Figure 13-7: The Advanced dialog box.

Figure 13-8: Only ad hoc networks are listed.

Share Files on the Ad Hoc Network

1. Open Windows Explorer or My Computer.

2. In the Address bar, enter two back slashes and then the name of the other computer, as shown in Figure 13-9.

3. Press the Enter key. A list of shared folders and resources appears. Open a shared folder to access it.

4. Use the Edit menu to cut, copy, and paste files over the network.

 To determine the name of a computer, right-click the My Computer icon and choose Properties. Click the Computer Name tab, and note the name listed next to Full Computer Name.

Disconnect from an Ad Hoc Network

1. Right-click the Wireless Connection icon in the Windows system tray.

2. Choose Disable from the menu shown in Figure 13-10.

 Disabling the wireless connection disables all wireless connections to the computer. If you want to disconnect from an ad hoc network and connect to an infrastructure network, double-click the Wireless Connection icon and click View Wireless Networks. Select the Ad Hoc Network and click Disconnect. Then choose an infrastructure network and click Connect.

3. On a Pocket PC, tap the Wi-Fi Connection icon on the Today screen, and then tap Turn Off in the WLAN Utility. To connect to a different network, tap Setting, tap-and-hold on the network to which you want to connect, and choose Connect.

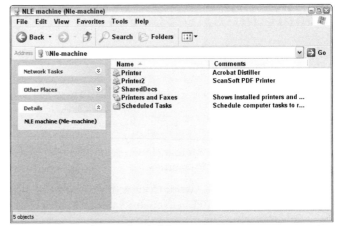

Figure 13-9: Enter the network path of the computer you want to access.

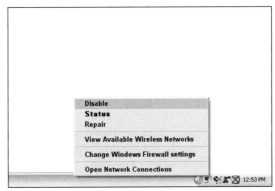

Figure 13-10: Disable the ad hoc connection.

Remove an Ad Hoc Connection

1. Choose Start⇨My Network Places.

2. Click View Network Connections under Network Tasks on the left side of the screen.

3. Right-click the wireless network adapter and choose Properties from the menu shown in Figure 13-11.

4. In the Wireless Network Connection Properties dialog box, click the Wireless Networks tab.

5. Select the ad hoc network, as shown in Figure 13-12.

6. Click Remove.

 If you know that you won't be connecting to any ad hoc connections for the foreseeable future, click Advanced and choose Access Point (Infrastructure) Networks Only to keep your computer secure from unauthorized ad hoc networks.

 To delete an ad hoc network from a Pocket PC, open the list of wireless networks in the Pocket PC WLAN utility. Tap-and-hold on the network you want to delete, and then choose Remove Settings from menu that appears.

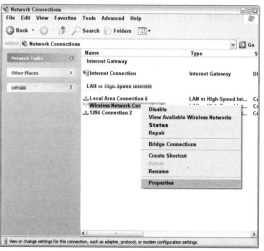

Figure 13-11: Right-click the wireless adapter and choose Properties.

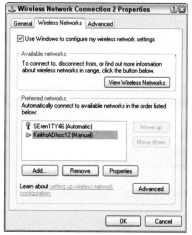

Figure 13-12: Remove unused ad hoc networks.

Troubleshoot an Ad Hoc Network

1. Make sure that the wireless adapter is active.

2. Right-click the Network Connection icon in the system tray and choose Repair from the menu shown in Figure 13-13.

3. Check that you are not currently connected to an infrastructure network. (If you are connected to an infrastructure network, disconnect from it.)

4. Make sure the SSID is correct and that each computer has the same SSID set.

 The SSID is usually case sensitive. If the SSID is incorrect, delete the ad hoc connection and make a new connection using the correct SSID.

5. Re-enter the WEP key (see Figure 13-14). Like SSIDs, the WEP key may be case sensitive.

6. Temporarily disable WEP encryption.

7. Temporarily disable your firewall/Internet security program.

 These troubleshooting steps help you resolve connectivity problems. Stop following the steps when the problem is resolved.

 For more information on how to disable WEP encryption, turn to Chapter 6. I go over how to disable a firewall in Chapter 7.

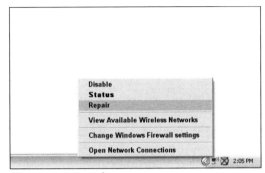

Figure 13-13: Repair the connection.

Figure 13-14: Double-check the WEP key and SSID.

Using Bluetooth Devices

Most wireless networks use 802.11b/g technologies, more commonly referred to as Wi-Fi (short for Wireless Fidelity). Bluetooth is another wireless networking technology that is increasing in popularity. Bluetooth signals usually have a maximum range of about 10 meters, making the technology less useful than Wi-Fi for creating wireless computer networks. However, Bluetooth is a great way to connect other kinds of devices, including:

➠ Cell phones

➠ Headsets

➠ PDAs

➠ GPS receivers

➠ Printers

➠ Keyboards and mice

These are just a few examples. New Bluetooth-compatible devices are becoming available. In this chapter, I show you how to connect to and use several common types of Bluetooth devices.

 Bluetooth radio waves can cause slight interference with 802.11b/g Wi-Fi signals. To reduce interference and improve the performance of both Wi-Fi and Bluetooth gear, try to position Bluetooth and Wi-Fi antennas as far apart from each other as possible.

Chapter 14

Get ready to . . .

Add Bluetooth to Your Windows PC

1. If your PC doesn't already have built-in Bluetooth, obtain a Bluetooth adapter (see Figure 14-1).

    The device should be compatible with your computer and easy to install. The USB adapter shown in Figure 14-1 easily connects to the USB port on any Windows PC.

2. Follow the device's instructions to install the drive software (see Figure 14-2).

    Usually you must install the driver software *before* you install or connect the Bluetooth adapter. I also strongly recommend that you check the Web site of the Bluetooth adapter's manufacturer to see if there are any updates. If your Bluetooth adapter is an internal expansion card, shut down the computer and install the card as described in the manufacturer's instructions. If your Bluetooth adapter connects to a USB port or cardbus slot, connect the adapter.

3. After Windows has finished updating and installing drivers, restart your computer.

4. After the computer is restarted, double-click the My Bluetooth Places icon on your Windows desktop, or double-click the Bluetooth icon in the Windows system tray.

    The system tray is the area in the lower-right corner of the screen next to the clock. The Bluetooth icon is (surprise) blue, with a white design on it that looks sort of like the letter B.

Figure 14-1: This Bluetooth adapter plugs into a USB port.

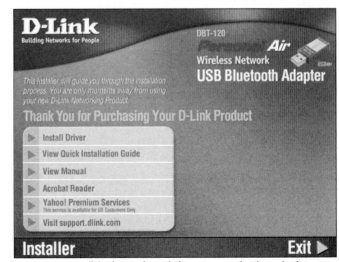

Figure 14-2: Install the driver software before connecting the Bluetooth adapter.

5. In the initial Bluetooth Configuration Wizard that appears, choose where you want Bluetooth icons to appear, and then click Next.

 You can have Bluetooth icons in the Windows Start menu, the Programs menu, and My Computer.

6. Enter a name for the computer, as shown in Figure 14-3, select the computer type, and click the Next button twice.

 The computer's name should be descriptive so that you can easily identify it from other Bluetooth-enabled devices.

7. In the next Bluetooth Service Selection screen, select services that will be offered by this computer by Bluetooth (see Figure 14-4).

 If you're not sure about the purpose of a particular service, click it to view a description. In Figure 14-4, I am viewing a description of the File Transfer service. You can also customize notification settings and other options for most services by clicking the Configure button next to each respective service.

8. Click the Next button and then click the Skip button to close the Bluetooth configuration wizard.

Figure 14-3: Give your computer a descriptive name.

Figure 14-4: Select the services you will offer.

Set Bluetooth Discovery Options

1. Right-click the Bluetooth icon in the Windows system tray and choose Advanced Configuration from the menu.

2. In the Bluetooth Configuration screen, click the Accessibility tab (see Figure 14-5).

3. Select the Let Other Bluetooth Devices Discover this Computer option.

    If you enable discovery, other Bluetooth computers will be able to see your computer. However, you can control access using the Allow menu below.

4. Click the Discovery tab (see Figure 14-6).

5. Select the Look for Other Bluetooth Devices option and choose how often you want to perform a check.

6. Click the Apply button and then click OK to close the Bluetooth Configuration dialog box.

    If you are going to be using your computer in public, you should turn off Bluetooth discovery (both incoming and outgoing) to prevent strangers from accessing your computer. Bluetooth *sniffer* programs — programs that scan for and identify active Bluetooth signals — are becoming increasingly popular. In fact, if you don't need your Bluetooth radio you should disable it or (if possible) remove any USB or cardbus Bluetooth adapters.

Figure 14-5: Enable Bluetooth discovery.

Figure 14-6: Let your computer discover other Bluetooth devices.

Connect to a Bluetooth Device from Windows

1. Double-click the My Bluetooth Places desktop icon or double-click the Bluetooth icon in the Windows system tray.

2. Click Search for Devices in Range under Bluetooth Tasks on the left side of the My Bluetooth Places window.

3. In the resulting list of Bluetooth devices that are currently active and in range, double-click a device to reveal a list of services available for that device (see Figure 14-7).

4. Double-click a service to start using it. (To create a direct connection for most devices, double-click the Serial Port service.)

 Windows make take a few seconds to configure port drivers for the device.

5. In the resulting Bluetooth PIN Code request dialog box (see Figure 14-8), enter a four-digit PIN code and then click OK.

6. Enter the same four-digit PIN on the other computer or device, if necessary.

 In some cases, a device's manufacturer tells you to use a specific PIN code such as 0000. Otherwise, make up your own PIN code. After you click OK in Windows, you may need to enter the same PIN code on the other device to create the partnership.

Figure 14-7: Bluetooth devices within range.

Figure 14-8: Enter a PIN code for the devices to share.

Add Bluetooth to Your Mac

1. If you are adding a USB Bluetooth adapter, start up your computer and then connect the adapter to an open USB port (see Figure 14-9).

    A Bluetooth icon appears on the menu bar in the lower-right corner next to the clock.

2. Click the Bluetooth icon in the menu bar and choose Open Bluetooth Preferences from the menu that appears.

3. On the Settings tab of the Bluetooth window, shown in Figure 14-10, select the Discoverable check box to allow other devices to discover your Mac.

    If you're using your iBook or PowerBook in a public location, it's a good idea to turn off Bluetooth to prevent strangers from accessing your computer. Click Turn Bluetooth Off to temporarily disable Bluetooth.

4. Choose whether you want to require authentication for connecting Bluetooth devices. Doing so enables you to use Bluetooth while keeping your computer more secure.

5. Choose whether you want the Bluetooth Setup Assistant to appear when no input device — such as a keyboard or mouse — is detected. This setting makes it easier to use Bluetooth input devices.

6. Close the Bluetooth window.

    Many newer Macs come with built-in Bluetooth adapters. Check your computer's documentation if you're not sure. Mac OS 10.2 or better is required for Bluetooth compatibility. With OS 10.2 or better, Bluetooth software is built-in to the operating system so no special installation is required.

Figure 14-9: Many Mac keyboards have a spare USB port.

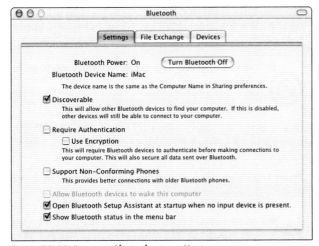

Figure 14-10: Setting up Bluetooth on your Mac is easy.

Connect a Bluetooth Device to Your Mac

1. Click the Bluetooth icon in the menu bar and choose Open Bluetooth Preferences from the menu that appears.

2. Click the Devices tab.

3. Click Pair New Device.

4. In the Pair with a Bluetooth Device dialog box, click the device with which you want to pair (see Figure 14-11).

 If you don't see the desired device listed, make sure it's turned on and in Pairing mode, and then click Search Again in the Pair with a Bluetooth Device dialog box. The device's documentation should include instructions for enabling pairing mode on the device.

5. Click the Pair button.

6. In the dialog box shown in Figure 14-12, enter a passkey and then click OK. The paired device is now listed on the Devices tab of your Bluetooth Preferences dialog box.

 In some cases, a device's manufacturer tells you to use a specific PIN code such as 0000. Otherwise, make up your own PIN code. You may also need to enter the same PIN code on the other device to create the partnership.

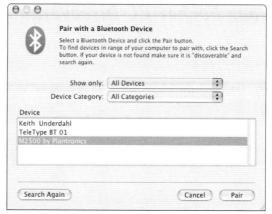

Figure 14-11: Pair your Mac to a Bluetooth device.

 To unpair a device, open the Bluetooth Preferences dialog box, open the Devices tab, select the device, and click Delete Pairing.

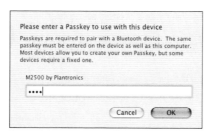

Figure 14-12: Enter a passkey.

Make Your Pocket PC Discoverable

1. Tap the Bluetooth icon on the Today screen to open the Bluetooth settings.

    Alternatively, choose Start⇨Settings, tap the Connections tab, and then tap Bluetooth.

2. Select the Turn on Bluetooth and Make this Device Discoverable to Other Devices option, as shown in Figure 14-13.

3. Tap OK to close the Settings screen.

Create a Pocket PC Partnership

1. Tap the Bluetooth icon on the Today screen to open the Bluetooth settings and then tap the Devices tab.

    Make sure the other device is on and in pairing mode.

2. Tap New Partnership.

3. Tap the name of the device to which you want to connect and then tap Next.

4. Enter a passkey (see Figure 14-14), and then tap Next.

5. Select services you want to use with the device and tap Save.

Figure 14-13: Enable the Bluetooth radio and discovery.

Figure 14-14: Enter a passkey.

Talk Wirelessly with a Bluetooth Headset

1. Create a partnership between your computer and the headset, as I describe earlier in this chapter.

2. Right-click the Bluetooth icon in the Windows system tray and choose Quick Connect⇨Headset and then choose the name of your headset (see Figure 14-15).

3. Launch the program with which you want to use the Bluetooth headset and then open the Options dialog box for that program (see Figure 14-16).

     In the example shown here, I am setting up my Bluetooth headset for use with Skype. Choose Tools⇨Options to open the Skype Options dialog box.

4. Select Bluetooth Audio for your input and output audio hardware.

5. Enable ringing on your PC speakers, if an option is available.

6. Place a test call to make sure that everything is working.

7. To disconnect the headset, right-click the Bluetooth system tray icon again, choose Quick Connect⇨ Headset⇨the name of your headset, and then click Yes when you are asked to confirm that you want to break the connection.

     In Skype, click the Make a Test Call to Skype Answering Machine link at the bottom of the Skype Options dialog box. See Chapter 24 for more on voice chatting with Skype.

Figure 14-15: Quick-connect to your Bluetooth headset.

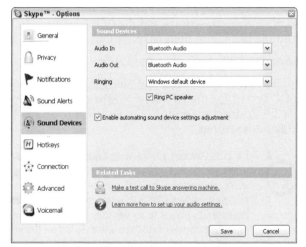

Figure 14-16: Choose Bluetooth Audio as your audio device.

Get Directions from a Bluetooth GPS Receiver

1. Tap the Bluetooth icon on the Today screen to open the Bluetooth settings and then tap the Devices tab.

2. Tap New Partnership and create a partnership with the GPS receiver, as I describe earlier in this chapter.

The passkey for a GPS receiver is usually 0000.

3. In the Bluetooth settings, tap the COM Ports tab to bring it to the front, and then tap New Outgoing Port.

4. Select the GPS receiver and tap Next.

5. In the Port drop-down menu (see Figure 14-17), choose a COM port for the GPS receiver. Do not check the Secure Connection option. Tap Finish and OK to close Bluetooth settings.

The exact COM port you use varies depending on both the GPS receiver and the Pocket PC you are using. Check the GPS manufacturer's documentation for COM port recommendations. In my example shown here, COM8 is the port to use to connect my Teletype Bluetooth GPS receiver to my Dell Axim X51. You may have to experiment with several COM ports before you find one that works.

6. Install your GPS mapping software, and then open the GPS settings in the mapping program.

7. Make sure that the mapping program has the correct COM port set for the GPS receiver (see Figure 14-18).

Figure 14-17: Select a COM port for the GPS receiver.

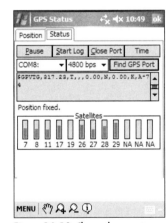

Figure 14-18: Choose the correct COM port.

8. Position the GPS receiver so that it is still and has a clear view of the sky.

> GPS receivers usually cannot get an initial fix on your position inside a building or under the metal roof of your car. However, after the position is fixed, you may have more flexibility on where you position the receiver.

9. Open your mapping program (see Figure 14-19), load some maps, and start navigating!

> These instructions assume you are using a Bluetooth GPS receiver with a Pocket PC. Most GPS receivers such as the Teletype receiver shown here can also be used with Windows PCs such as laptops.

Figure 14-19: The GPS receiver shows your current position.

Networking Wirelessly with Your Pocket PC

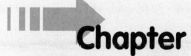

1 probably don't have to tell you how rapidly computers have advanced in the last couple of decades, while at the same time getting smaller and easier to use. Nowhere is this more evident than in the latest Pocket PCs, which pack more computing power than Apollo astronauts took to the moon. Believe it or not, even the computer running the modern International Space Station is far less powerful than the typical Pocket PC. With a Pocket PC, you can check e-mail, browse the Web, store contacts, run PowerPoint presentations, navigate with GPS mapping programs, and more.

Many new Pocket PCs also contain Wi-Fi or Bluetooth wireless networking technologies. This chapter shows you how to use your Pocket PC untethered from cradles and synchronization cables. I go over how to:

➡ Make Bluetooth connections between your Pocket PC and other computers (including other Pocket PCs).

➡ Beam files or use ActiveSync with Bluetooth.

➡ Set up and use wireless network connections between your Pocket PC and Wi-Fi networks.

➡ Ensure that wireless networking doesn't put too much of a strain on your Pocket PC's battery.

 The steps in this chapter assume you have a Pocket PC running the Windows Mobile 5 operating system or newer.

Make a Bluetooth Connection

1. Tap Start⇨Settings and then tap the Connections tab.

2. Tap the Bluetooth icon to open the Bluetooth connection panel.

3. Turn on Bluetooth and enable discovery, as shown in Figure 15-1.

4. Tap the Devices tab and then tap New Partnership.

5. In the list of devices that appears (see Figure 15-2), tap the name of the device to which you want to connect, and then tap Next.

 If the desired computer or device isn't listed, make sure it is discoverable or in pairing mode and then tap Refresh.

6. Enter a passkey and then tap Next.

 Computers usually require a unique passkey, but devices like headsets and GPS receivers usually use the passkey 0000.

7. Select services you want to use with the device and tap Save.

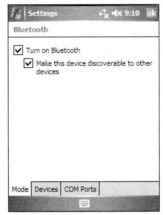

Figure 15-1: Enable Bluetooth and Bluetooth discovery.

Figure 15-2: Choose the device to which you want to connect.

Beam Files with Bluetooth

1. Locate an item that you want to beam.

    You can select contacts in your contacts list, appointments in your calendar, images in the picture viewer, files in File Explorer, and many other items.

2. Choose Menu⇨Beam (see Figure 15-3). The Pocket PC searches for a device to which the item can be beamed.

    In Figure 15-3, the menu option says Beam Picture because I am preparing to beam a picture. The Beam selection is contextual and changes depending on the type of item you are beaming.

3. In the resulting list, tap the device to which you want to beam the item (see Figure 15-4). The file is beamed to the device.

    Beaming is most useful for quickly sending items between Pocket PCs.

    To beam files from a desktop PC to a Pocket PC, use the Bluetooth Exchange folder in your Windows My Documents folder.

Figure 15-3: Choose Beam from the program's menu.

Figure 15-4: Select the device to which you want to beam the item.

Use ActiveSync with Bluetooth

1. Install the ActiveSync software on a desktop or laptop computer that is equipped with a Bluetooth receiver.

2. On your Pocket PC, tap Start⇨Programs.

3. Tap the ActiveSync icon to open the ActiveSync program.

4. Choose Menu⇨Connect via Bluetooth, as shown in Figure 15-5.

Make a Wi-Fi Connection

1. Tap Start⇨Settings and then tap the Connections tab.

2. Tap the icon for the WLAN utility and then tap Setting.

3. Tap the Network Adapters tab and then tap the name of your Pocket PC's wireless adapter.

4. On the IP Address tab, select Use Server-Assigned IP Address, as shown in Figure 15-6.

The network's DHCP server will assign an IP address to your Pocket PC when you connect to the wireless network.

5. Tap OK to close the wireless adapter settings window.

6. Tap the Wireless tab to bring it to the front.

Figure 15-5: Configure ActiveSync to connect via Bluetooth.

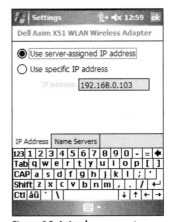

Figure 15-6: Let the server assign an IP address to your Pocket PC.

7. Tap the name of the Wireless network to which you want to connect.

 If the network isn't listed, tap Add New. In the Windows Mobile 5 operating system, the configuration window that opens does not have a Cancel button or link. Therefore, if you tap Add New but then do not have a network SSID or other information to add, you must soft-reset the Pocket PC to get rid of the window. Most Pocket PCs have a soft reset button on the back; check the manufacturer's documentation for soft reset instructions.

8. On the General tab, enter the network's SSID in the Network Name field, if it isn't already filled in.

9. Tap the Network Key tab and choose WEP in the Data Encryption menu if the network uses WEP encryption. If the network doesn't use any encryption, skip ahead to Step 11.

10. If the network uses WEP encryption, enter the network key (see Figure 15-7).

11. Tap OK to save your settings.

12. Close all open windows. If you have a successful connection you will see a green stair-step wireless connection icon in the lower-right corner of the Today screen.

 Tap the Wireless Connection icon to quickly open Wi-Fi settings.

13. If you're not sure which wireless network your Pocket PC is connected to, tap the Connectivity icon on the menu bar, as shown in Figure 15-8.

Figure 15-7: Enter network encryption settings.

Figure 15-8: Tap the Connectivity icon.

Share Files with a Network Computer

1. Use File Explorer to locate a file you want to copy.

     To open File Explorer, tap Start➪Programs and then tap the File Explorer icon.

2. Select the file you want to copy and choose Menu➪ Edit➪Copy.

3. Tap Menu➪Open Path➪New Path.

4. Type the name of a network computer to which you want to connect, as shown in Figure 15-9.

     The name of the computer should be preceded by two back slashes, as shown in Figure 15-9.

5. Tap OK.

6. Enter a valid user name and password for a user account on the computer to which you are trying to connect, and tap OK again.

     If you just want to connect to shared public folders on the computer, leave the user name and password fields blank. After tapping OK you may be asked whether you want to save the password.

7. In the list of available folders and items, tap a folder or other item to open it (see Figure 15-10).

8. Choose Menu➪Edit➪Paste to copy the file from your Pocket PC to the network computer.

Figure 15-9: Connect to another computer.

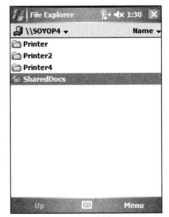

Figure 15-10: Tap a folder name to open it.

Browse the Web at a Hotspot

1. Tap the Wi-Fi connection icon in the lower-right corner of the Today screen.

    If the Wi-Fi adapter is not enabled, tap Turn On.

2. Tap Setting and wait for the hotspot's signal to appear in the list of networks (see Figure 15-11).

3. Tap the connection and enter a network key if one is required.

4. Tap OK until all of the settings dialog boxes are closed.

5. When the Wi-Fi Connection icon turns green, tap Start⇨ Internet Explorer.

6. If you are required to log into the hotspot, type the log in URL in the Address bar and tap Enter. Follow the hotspot's instructions to log in.

7. Once logged in, browse the Web normally, as shown in Figure 15-12.

    Some hotspots require you to pay for access, so the log-in URL may have instructions and payment options. Public hotspots often require no log-in, although some do require that you create a free account and log-in because free access is limited.

    Remember, when you use a public hotspot anyone else using the hotspot could access your computer. If you use hotspots frequently and your computer contains sensitive data, consider installing a security program specifically designed for Pocket PCs.

Figure 15-11: Select the hotspot network.

Figure 15-12: Browsing the Web from a hotspot is easy!

Adjust Power Options

1. Tap Start⇨Settings, and then tap the Connections tab.

2. Tap the icon for the WLAN utility.

3. Choose a WLAN power save mode:

    • **Enable:** Wi-Fi radio power is reduced to preserve battery power.

    • **Disable:** Wi-Fi radio power is used at the greatest possible power for best range.

    • **Auto:** Wi-Fi radio power changes dynamically based on your usage.

4. To prevent lost data, select the Disable WLAN to conserve power when battery is low option, as shown in Figure 15-13.

Figure 15-13: Adjust Wi-Fi settings to stretch the life of your battery.

Keep Your Pocket PC Secure

1. Tap Start⇨Settings and then tap the Password icon. Create a password that must be entered after a period of inactivity, as shown in Figure 15-14.

     A password prevents someone else from using the Pocket PC to access your network, in the unfortunate event that the Pocket PC is lost or stolen.

2. Install a security program specifically designed for your version of the Windows Mobile operating system.

3. Disable Bluetooth and Wi-Fi when not in use.

Figure 15-14: Secure your Pocket PC with a password.

Part V
Practical Applications

The 5th Wave — By Rich Tennant

"That's it! We're getting a wireless network for the house."

Project: Creating a Network Bridge

*F*or thousands of years, people have built bridges to connect separated land areas. When you create a home network, you can build a bridge between two different kinds of networks, namely wired and wireless networks.

Suppose you already have an established Ethernet wired network, and you have just purchased a single Wi-Fi-equipped laptop that you want to use with your network. You could buy a new router/wireless access point (WAP), but that's expensive and complicated to set up. Alternatively, you could just add a wireless adapter to one of your existing Ethernet wired computers, and then use this computer as a virtual bridge between your Wi-Fi laptop and your Ethernet network.

In this chapter, you find out how to:

➠ Turn a computer into a network bridge.

➠ Add a wireless adapter to a computer.

➠ Set up the adapters to create the bridge.

 For more details on basic wireless network settings, see Chapters 1. Chapter 2 covers wireless adapter settings, and Chapter 6 shows how to set up wireless network security.

Install a Wireless Adapter on the Bridging Computer

1. Shut down your computer and unplug its power cable.

2. Determine whether your computer can support an internal Wi-Fi card. You should have at least one open PCI slot. The computer shown in Figure 16-1 has four open PCI slots.

    The slots in Figure 16-1 are PCI slots. If you are not familiar with computer hardware or if your computer is still under warranty, have a computer professional check your computer and perform the installation. Computer hardware is fragile and easily damaged.

3. If you have an open PCI slot and are willing to install an internal card, purchase and install an internal Wi-Fi card. Don't remove your Ethernet card; when you're done your computer should have both Ethernet and wireless network adapters, as shown in Figure 16-2.

4. If your computer does not have an empty PCI slot, or if you don't want to open the case and install an internal card, purchase an external Wi-Fi adapter that plugs into a USB port.

    Some external Wi-Fi adapters plug into a computer's Ethernet port. Don't get one of these unless your computer already has two Ethernet ports. Remember, you need at least one Ethernet port to connect to the rest of the Ethernet network and create your network bridge.

    A laptop can also be used as a network bridge. Connect the laptop's Ethernet port to the Ethernet network; then install a cardbus Wi-Fi adapter or use the laptop's built-in Wi-Fi if it is so equipped.

Figure 16-1: Open PCI slots.

Figure 16-2: The bridging computer should have both Ethernet and Wi-Fi adapters.

Configure the Wireless Adapter

1. Install the Wi-Fi adapter's driver software.

    See Chapter 3 for details on how to install the Wi-Fi adapter's driver software.

2. Choose Start⇨My Network Places.

3. On the left side of the My Network Places window, click View Network Connections.

4. Right-click the Wireless Network Connection and choose Properties from the menu that appears, as shown in Figure 16-3.

5. In the Wireless Network Connection Properties dialog box, click the Wireless Networks tab to bring it to the front.

    If you don't see the Wireless Networks tab, you may need to close the Properties dialog box and activate the wireless network connection. To activate the connection, right-click the connection in the Network Connections window and choose Enable.

6. Click Advanced.

7. Select Computer-to-computer (ad hoc) networks only, as shown in Figure 16-4 and click Close.

8. Set up an ad hoc network connection between the bridge computer and your other wireless computer, as described in Chapter 13.

Figure 16-3: Open the Properties dialog box for the wireless connection.

Figure 16-4: Choose ad hoc networks only.

Bridge the Connections

1. Choose Start⇨My Network Places.

2. On the left side of the My Network Places window, click View Network Connections.

3. Hold down the CTRL key on your keyboard and click once on your Ethernet network connection and then click once on your wireless connection so that both are selected, as shown in Figure 16-5.

     You can bridge any two or more network connections that are not being used for Internet connection sharing. For example, if one network connection connects directly to a broadband modem, you cannot bridge it to other network connections. In that case, you can simply use Internet Connection Sharing (described in Chapter 2) to share the broadband Internet connection with the rest of your network.

4. Right-click the computer's Ethernet network connection and choose Bridge Connections, as shown in Figure 16-6.

     The bridging process takes a few seconds. When the process is complete, a new Network Bridge category appears in your list of network connections. The Network Bridge category contains the network bridge as well as the two bridged connections.

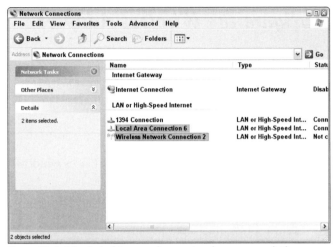

Figure 16-5: Select both of the network connections that you want to bridge.

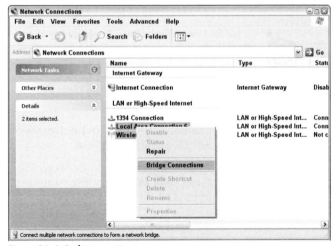

Figure 16-6: Bridge connections.

Adjust Bridge Settings

1. Choose Start➪My Network Places.

2. On the left side of the My Network Places window, click View Network Connections.

3. Right-click the Network Bridge listing and choose Properties, as shown in Figure 16-7.

4. In the Properties dialog box, add or remove a network adapter from the bridge (select or deselect) in the Adapters list, as shown in Figure 16-8.

     If a network adapter is installed on your computer but does not appear in the Adapters list, that adapter is not eligible for bridging.

5. In the lower portion of the General tab of the Network Bridge Properties dialog box, select which services you want to use with the bridge.

     For example, if you do not want to allow file sharing over the bridge, uncheck File and Printer Sharing for Microsoft Networks.

6. Click OK to save your changes and close the Network Bridge Properties dialog box.

Figure 16-7: The bridge is listed with other network connections.

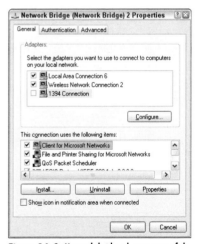

Figure 16-8: Network bridges have many of the same settings as other network connections.

Tear Down a Network Bridge

1. Choose Start⇨My Network Places.

2. On the left side of the My Network Places window, click View Network Connections.

3. Do one of the following:

    - To remove a single network adapter from a bridge, open the Properties dialog box for the network bridge and uncheck the desired connection as described in the previous section.

    - To temporarily disable a bridge, right-click the bridge and choose Disable as shown in Figure 16-9.

    - To permanently remove the bridge from your list of network connections, right-click the Network Bridge and choose Delete.

Figure 16-9: Disable or delete the bridge.

Project: Networking a Game Console

*W*ireless networking isn't just for computers. Another increasingly popular use for wireless networks is gaming with video game consoles, such as the Xbox or PlayStation. Modern game consoles can network with each other for linked-system play, and with a service like Xbox Live they can even connect to the Internet where you can play against people from all over the world.

Most modern game consoles have a built-in Ethernet port for networking. But if you don't want to run Ethernet cables all over your house, you can buy a Wi-Fi bridge that connects to your console and allows the console to use your wireless network.

In this chapter, you discover how to add wireless networking capabilities to an Xbox and then use it to play with other Xbox consoles in your home or online using Xbox Live.

To add a game console to your wireless network, you need to know the SSID, encryption settings, and security keys for your network. See Chapter 1 for information on logging in to your wireless access point and collection network information, and see Chapter 6 for more on wireless network security.

Add a Wireless Adapter to Your Console

1. Select a wireless adapter specifically designed for your game console.

    In theory, any Wi-Fi bridge that connects to an Ethernet port should work with your game console. In practice, however, if the adapter doesn't come with a setup disc to help you install and configure wireless network settings on the console, you may find it difficult or impossible to use.

2. Collect the SSID, encryption format, and encryption keys for your network and keep them handy.

    You need this information when you configure your wireless game adapter. See Chapters 1 and 2 for more information on how to obtain this information around your network.

3. Turn on the power on your game console and remove any game discs.

4. Connect the power cable to the wireless adapter; then connect an Ethernet cable between the adapter and the game console's Ethernet port.

5. Insert the wireless adapter's setup disc in the game console and close the tray.

6. If your wireless network is detected (see Figure 17-1), choose it and press A. Otherwise, choose Other and press A.

7. Enter your network's SSID as the network name (see Figure 17-2).

    The SSID is case sensitive, so make sure you enter it correctly here.

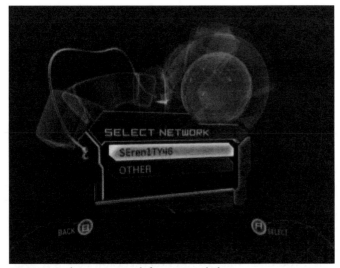

Figure 17-1: Choose your network if it appears in the list.

Figure 17-2: Enter your network's SSID.

8. On the Wireless Settings screen, shown in Figure 17-3, choose Security Type and press A.

9. Choose the security type used by your network (see Figure 17-4) and then press A.

 Most game console adapters are not compatible with WPA encryption.

10. Enter the encryption key and then choose Done.

11. On the Wireless Settings screen, choose Save and press A.

12. Check the status of your connection on the Wireless Status screen.

 The Wireless Status screen shows your connection speed and signal strength. If the signal strength is poor, try repositioning the wireless adapter so that it is high and not blocked by large furniture or other obstructions.

 If you are unable to create a successful connection, double-check that the SSID, encryption format, and encryption keys are entered correctly. In your router, temporarily disable WPA or WPA-PSK encryption if it is enabled.

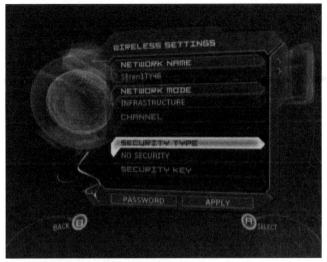

Figure 17-3: Adjust network security settings.

Figure 17-4: Choose your network's security type.

Adjust Wireless Network Settings

1. Turn on your game console, but make sure the disc is empty.

2. Choose Settings, as shown in Figure 17-5, and press A.

    If you have Xbox Live installed, choose Main Menu on the Xbox Live menu to reveal the menu shown in Figure 17-5.

3. In the Settings menu, choose Network Settings and press A.

4. In Network Settings, choose Advanced and press A.

5. Choose Wireless and press A to reveal the Wireless Status screen shown in Figure 17-6.

6. Choose Settings to open the Wireless Settings screen. There you can change the SSID, security type, and encryption key used by your network.

7. When you are done, choose Save on the Wireless Settings screen and press A to save your changes.

    If you ever change your network's SSID or encryption key, you will need to adjust wireless settings in your game console as well.

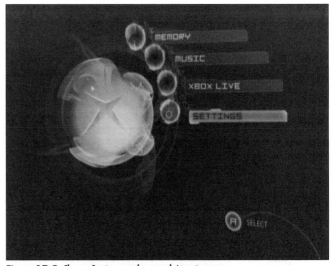

Figure 17-5: Choose Settings on the console's main menu.

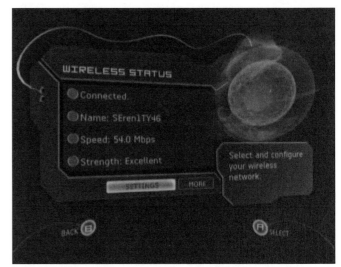

Figure 17-6: Choose Settings to change the wireless SSID and encryption keys.

Create an Ad Hoc Network between Consoles

1. Turn on your game console, but make sure that the disc is empty.

2. Choose Settings (refer to Figure 17-5) and press A.

    If you have Xbox Live installed, choose Main Menu on the Xbox Live menu to reveal the menu shown in Figure 17-5.

3. In the Settings menu, choose Network Settings and press A, and then in Network Settings, choose Advanced and press A again.

4. Choose Wireless and press A to reveal the Wireless Status screen. Choose Network Mode and press A.

5. Choose Ad Hoc as shown in Figure 17-7 and press A.

6. On the Wireless Status screen, choose Network Name and enter a name (SSID) for your ad hoc network.

    Each console must have the same network name. The network name should be different from the SSID for any other wireless network in broadcast range.

7. Select Security Type and choose No Security as your security type.

    Data encryption generally is not necessary when creating an ad hoc network between game consoles since no personal information or sensitive data is stored on the consoles.

8. On the Wireless Status screen, choose Apply (see Figure 17-8) and press A. Make sure each console has the same settings.

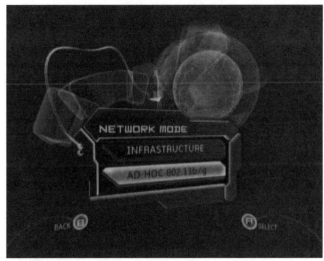

Figure 17-7: Choose Ad Hoc as your network mode.

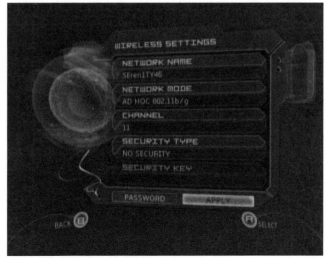

Figure 17-8: Apply the same settings on each console.

Connect to Xbox Live

1. Purchase and install an Xbox Live subscription kit.

    Xbox Live subscription kits are available at most electronics and video game retailers. You need a valid credit card when you create an Xbox live account, even though you won't need to make an online purchase if your subscription kit contains a valid subscription.

2. If your Xbox doesn't log in to Xbox Live automatically when you turn it on, remove any disc from the tray and choose Xbox Live from the main menu, as shown in Figure 17-9.

3. Choose your Xbox Live account, as shown in Figure 17-10, or choose New Account if you want to create a new account.

4. In the Xbox Live menu, choose Account Management to update your subscription or change other account settings.

    XBox Live requires a broadband (DSL or better) Internet connection. Make sure that you have a broadband Internet connection and a means to connect your Xbox to your network to share the Internet connection before buying and installing Xbox Live.

    If a game is compatible with XBox Live, it should log in and allow online play automatically. If XBox Live doesn't work, check the status of your XBox's network connection as shown earlier in this chapter, and also double-check that your XBox Live subscription is up to date. Subscriptions must usually be renewed annually.

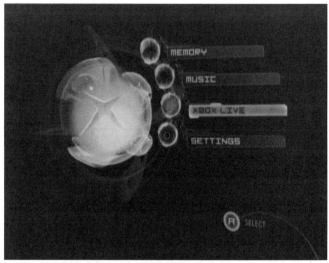

Figure 17-9: Choose Xbox Live from the main Xbox menu.

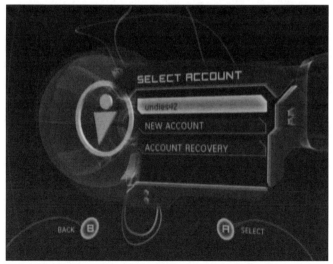

Figure 17-10: Select your current account here, or create a new account.

Project: Setting Up a Wireless Media Center

Your high-tech, Wi-Fi-equipped home just isn't complete without a wireless media center. With a wireless media center, you can use one computer to store and organize all of your music and video, and then stream that media wirelessly to any location in your home. With the right hardware, a wireless media center can also:

- Act as a TV tuner, allowing you to watch your favorite broadcast, satellite, or cable shows.

- Serve as a digital video recorder (DVR), recording shows onto a hard drive where they can be retrieved and watched later.

- Integrate with your TV and home entertainment system to provide an advanced, high-fidelity multimedia entertainment center.

This chapter shows you how to set up and use a computer as a wireless media center. Of course, the easiest way to set up a media center is to buy a purpose-built Media center PC running Windows Media Center Edition. But if you want to set up a computer yourself, the first section of this chapter provides general guidance on how to choose components (or a computer with the right components) and how to get the computer ready for multimedia.

Build a Media Center Computer

1. Select a modern processor with a speed greater than 2 GHz.

    Try to stick with an Intel Pentium 4 or better, or AMD Athlon XP or better. If you prefer Macs, most modern PowerMacs, iMacs, or MacMinis with a G4 or better processor should be adequate.

2. Choose a case that is attractive and designed for quiet operation. You don't want to listen to noisy computer fans while you try to watch DVD movies.

3. Make sure that the power supply provides at least 300 watts of power. High-quality display adapters, hard drives, and TV tuner cards use a lot of power.

    Several companies now offer fanless power supplies. A fanless power supply makes the computer a lot quieter.

4. Choose a motherboard with plenty of available PCI slots. The motherboard shown in Figure 18-1 has four open PCI slots.

5. Choose a high-quality video card with lots of dedicated video memory and video outputs that is compatible with your TV monitor.

    The next task in this chapter shows how to connect a TV to your video card.

6. Install TV tuner cards for both analog and HDTV signals. Some TV tuner cards support both HD and analog signals, such as the ADS Tech Instant HDTV PCI card shown in Figure 18-2.

Figure 18-1: Four open PCI slots.

Figure 18-2: The ADS Tech Instant HDTV PCI card.
Photo courtesy ADS Tech Inc., USA.

7. Select a high-quality sound card that supports 6.1 or 7.1 surround sound.

8. Connect the audio output on your sound card to the audio inputs on your home theater receiver to control the speakers, (see Figure 18-3).

 Most electronics stores sell cables that connect the mini-jack outputs on your sound card to the RCA-style analog audio inputs on a home theater receiver.

 This section provides only a basic overview of the features you want when you buy or build a media center computer. For detailed instructions on building and upgrading computers check out *Upgrading & Fixing PCs For Dummies* by Andy Rathbone (Wiley Publishing, Inc.).

Connect a TV to the Media Center

1. Determine the type of input cable that your TV will accept.

2. Connect one of the following types of cables between the TV's video input and the computer's video output:

- **Component:** These consist of three RCA-like connectors colored red, green, and blue and provide the best possible video quality.

- **S-Video:** This connector (see Figure 18-4) is more common and provides a high quality image.

- **Composite:** This yellow RCA-style connector (see Figure 18-4) provides good video quality, but is inferior to Component or S-Video.

 S-Video connectors carry only video images, and no sound. S-Video is preferable to composite video because S-Video offers higher picture quality.

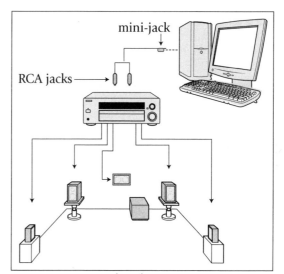

Figure 18-3: Connect to a home theater receiver.

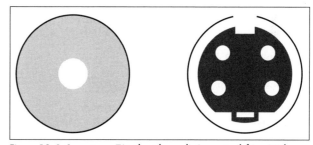

Figure 18-4: Connect your TV to the video card's Composite (left) or S-Video connector (right).

Watch DVDs

1. Insert a DVD movie into your computer's DVD-ROM drive.

2. When the auto-play window appears, shown in Figure 18-5, choose Play DVD Video using Windows Media Player and click OK.

    If the auto-play window doesn't appear, open Windows Media Player from the Start menu. When Windows Media Player opens, choose Play⇨DVD.

    If the DVD is recognized by Windows Media Player and begins to play, skip ahead to Step 8.

3. If Windows Media Player does not recognize the DVD, choose Tools⇨Download⇨Plug-ins.

4. On the Microsoft Web site, click the link for DVD Decoder Plug-ins, and then click the link to install the Windows XP Video Decoder Checkup Utility.

5. Follow the instructions on the Microsoft Web site to download and install the Windows XP Video Decoder Checkup Utility.

6. Choose Start⇨All Programs⇨Windows Media⇨ Microsoft Windows XP Video Decoder Checkup Utility.

7. Make sure your computer has at least one DVD decoder installed. Figure 18-6 shows that the computer has four DVD decoders installed.

8. If your computer doesn't have a DVD decoder, return to the Microsoft Windows Media Player Plug-ins page as described in Step 3, and then download and install one of the DVD decoder programs listed on the Web site.

Figure 18-5: Play the DVD.

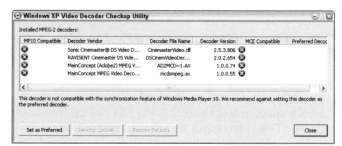

Figure 18-6: Make sure your computer has a DVD decoder installed.

9. To play the movie at full-screen, press Alt+Enter. Press Alt+Enter again (or press Esc) to leave the full-screen mode.

10. Use the DVD controls at the bottom of the screen (see Figure 18-7) to control playback.

The menu bar at the top of the screen and the toolbar at the bottom of the screen only appear when you move the computer's mouse. If you leave the mouse still for several seconds, the bars will disappear, leaving only the movie image on the screen.

11. To gain access to DVD features such as language tracks or the DVD root menu, right-click the image, as shown in Figure 18-7.

If you have a Macintosh with a DVD-ROM drive, your computer already has a built-in DVD decoder. No other decoder installation is necessary to watch DVDs.

Organize Media Files

1. Store all of your media files on a second hard drive. (If your computer has only one hard drive, use the Shared (Mac OS X) or Shared Documents (Windows) folder to store your media.)

2. Create root-level folders for storing audio, video, images, and other media, as shown in Figure 18-8.

3. Within each folder, create subfolders to further organize your media.

For audio, create subfolders for each artist. For still images, create subfolders by subject or a given time period.

4. Copy and paste media into appropriate folders on the hard drive.

Figure 18-7: Access DVD features.

Figure 18-8: Organize all of your media.

Share Media with the Network from Windows

1. In My Computer or Windows Explorer, right-click the root-level folder in which you store all of your media, and choose Sharing and Security from the menu that appears.

 If you use a separate hard drive exclusively for storing media, right-click the drive letter in My Computer or Windows Explorer. Do not share an entire hard drive if it contains program files or documents that you don't want to share.

2. Under Network Sharing and Security, select the Share This Folder on the Network check box, as shown in Figure 18-9.

3. Give the folder a share name. Other network computers see this name when they access the shared disk or folder.

 Do not select the Allow Network Users to Change My Files option. This prevents others from accidentally deleting your songs and other media.

4. Click OK to apply your changes and close the Properties dialog box.

5. In My Computer or Windows Explorer, make sure that the shared folder or disk has a hand on its icon, as shown in Figure 18-10. The hand indicates that the folder is shared.

Figure 18-9: Share your media store folder with the network.

Figure 18-10: The disk is shared with your network.

Share Media with the Network from Mac OS X

1. Choose Apple⇨System Preferences and then open the Sharing icon.

2. Select Personal File Sharing (see Figure 18-11) to allow file sharing with other computers. If you plan to share media with Windows PCs, also perform the following:

   • Select Windows Sharing.

   • Click the Enable Accounts button and then select the user account or accounts that you want to use when accessing your Mac from a Windows PC.

 If you see a yellow warning triangle next to Windows Sharing, as shown in Figure 18-11, you still need to enable at least one user account to log-in from Windows. See Chapter 4 for more on sharing files between Windows and Mac OS X.

3. Close System Preferences.

4. Open the Finder, and then browse to the folder containing the media you want to share.

5. Select the folder you want to share and press CMD+I.

6. In the Info dialog box that appears for the folder, click the arrow next to Ownership and Permissions (see Figure 18-12), and then click the arrow next to Details Under Ownership and Permissions.

7. Choose Everyone in the Group menu and then choose Read Only in the Access menu.

8. Click Apply to enclosed items and then close the Info dialog box.

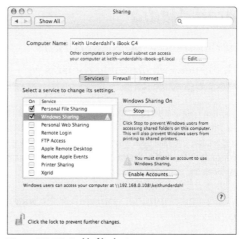

Figure 18-11: Enable file sharing on your computer.

Figure 18-12: Press CMD+I to set folder permissions.

Access Shared Media

1. In Windows, choose Start⇨My Network Places.

2. Double-click the network place that contains your media files (see Figure 18-13).

 If you don't see the network folder containing your media, click View Workgroup Computers on the left side of the My Network Places window, and then open the icon for the workgroup computer which contains the media. Remember, the media server computer must be on and connected to the network.

3. Open the folder and subfolder containing the media you want to play.

4. To play a song or movie, double-click it (see Figure 18-14).

5. To play multiple files or folder, hold down the Ctrl key and click once on each file or folder that you want to play, and then click Play All or Play Selection under Video Tasks or Audio Tasks on the left side of the window.

 When you play music on a Macintosh from a network location, iTunes first copies the song to the local computer before playing it. To change this behavior, open iTunes and choose iTunes⇨ Preferences. Click Advanced at the top of the Preferences window, and then deselect the Copy files to iTunes Music folder when adding to library option.

 Disable power-saving settings on the media server. If the server shuts down its hard drives or goes to sleep after a period of inactivity, other network computers won't be able to access media files stored on the server.

Figure 18-13: Locate the network folder containing your media files.

Figure 18-14: Double-click some media to play it locally.

Watch TV on the Computer

1. Install a TV tuner card that supports the type of TV signal you want to watch.

    Some TV tuner cards support newer HD (High Definition) TV signals, while others support analog TV. Most over-the-air broadcast signals are analog, although many TV stations now also offer HD broadcast as well. If you have cable or satellite TV, check the provider's documentation to find out what technologies are available to you. In this example I am using an ADS Tech (www.adstech.com) InstantHDTV card which supports both HD and analog signals.

2. Connect all appropriate antennas or cables to the tuner card.

3. Install tuner software such as SnapStream's Beyond TV (`www.snapstream.com`).

    When you install the software, the setup program should gather information about your location and cable system. This information is then used to provide a program guide which is accurate for your location.

4. Launch the tuner software and enter the program guide (see Figure 18-15).

5. Select a program and click it to watch it (see Figure 18-16).

    If you have a media center remote, use its controls to manipulate the program guide and playback. Press Info on the media center remote to view details about the current program.

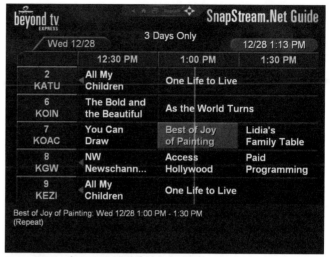

Figure 18-15: A live program guide for broadcast TV.

Figure 18-16: View program details.

Record Live TV

1. Launch the tuner program on your media center computer and open the program guide.

2. Locate a show in the program guide that you want to record.

3. Click the show you want to record and choose the Record This Episode option, as shown in Figure 18-17.

4. To manage recordings, return to the main menu and click Setup Recordings.

5. Click Setup Recordings in the Recordings menu, and then click Upcoming Recordings to review a list of upcoming recordings.

6. Click a show to view recording commands (see Figure 18-18). Choose the Do Not Record option to cancel a scheduled recording.

To immediately begin recording a show that you are currently watching, either press the Record button on your media center remote, or click on the live TV display and then click the Record button that appears in the control menu. In SnapStream Beyond TV, the control menu is in the upper-right corner.

Other tuner programs may differ slightly, but the basic concept and controls should be the same.

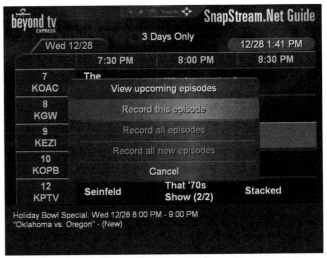

Figure 18-17: Locate a show that you want to record.

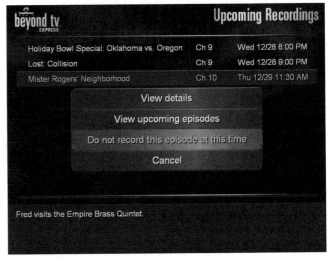

Figure 18-18: Manage scheduled recordings.

Play Recorded TV

1. Open the main menu of your TV tuner and recording program.

2. Choose Recorded Shows in the main menu

3. Select a program in the list of recorded shows (see Figure 18-19).

4. Click Play to play the program (see Figure 18-20).

5. Click Delete to delete the program.

By default, recorded shows are kept on the hard drive until space is needed. If you want to save a show indefinitely, click Keep Until and then choose Keep Until I Delete It in the menu that appears.

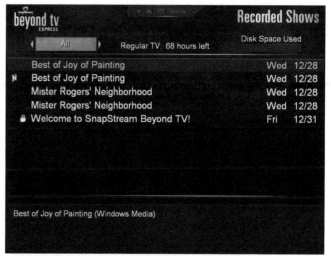

Figure 18-19: Choose Recorded Shows from the main menu.

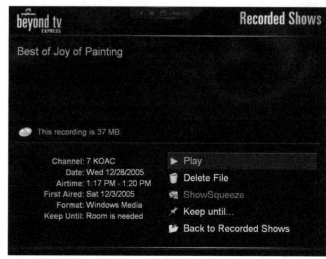

Figure 18-20: Play or delete the recording.

Project: Adding Wireless Network Storage

*N*etworks enable you to easily share resources with all of your computers. The most commonly shared resources are Internet connections, printers, and files. Throughout this book, I show how to share all of these things, including files that are stored on individual computers.

If you do a lot of file sharing, you should consider a dedicated network storage drive. Many companies now offer hard drive enclosures that connect directly to your network, either wirelessly or by Ethernet connection. The benefits of network storage include:

➠ All of your computers can easily share commonly used files such as music, videos, and photos.

➠ You don't have to leave unused computers turned on simply because you may want to access files that are stored on their hard drives.

In this chapter, you find out how to set up and use a wireless network storage drive on your home network.

Choose a Network Storage Device

1. Decide whether you want a network storage drive with built-in Wi-Fi (see Figure 19-1).

    Most network storage drives connect to the network via Ethernet. Ethernet connections are usually easy to configure and offer greater data transfer speed, but wireless storage drives provide a bit more flexibility in where you position and how you use the drive.

2. Choose whether or not you need a network storage device with a built-in hard drive.

    Most network storage devices have a built-in hard drive, but some devices are simply enclosures into which you can install your own hard drive. In the following task, I go over how to install a hard drive in a network storage enclosure.

Install a Hard Drive

1. Open the enclosure as described in the manufacturer's instructions.

    These instructions only apply if you purchased a network storage enclosure that does not include a hard drive. Consult the documentation that came with your storage enclosure for special instructions and requirements.

2. Prepare the hard drive for installation in the enclosure.

3. Connect a hard drive cable (the connector looks like Figure 19-2) between the hard drive and the hard drive enclosure.

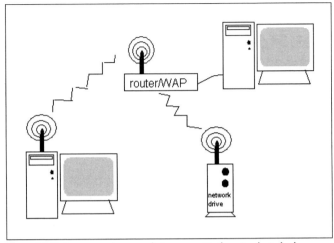

Figure 19-1: Some network storage devices connect to the network wirelessly.

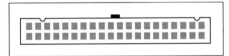

Figure 19-2: Hard drive cables usually use EIDE connectors.

 Most network storage enclosures use EIDE drives. Only install a new, blank drive in the enclosure. If it has a jumper for setting the drive mode, set the jumper to Master. The next section of this chapter shows how to format the hard drive.

Install the Management Software

1. Connect the power cable to your network storage drive and then turn on its power.

2. Connect an Ethernet cable between the network drive and your router.

    Even if your network drive has built-in wireless capability, it is necessary to connect an Ethernet cable for initial setup. When you are done configuring the drive, you can disconnect the Ethernet cable and reposition the drive. Make sure that the DHCP server in your router is configured and running properly, so it can assign an IP address to the network drive.

3. Insert the drive's setup utility disc in the CD-ROM drive of one of your network computers, and run the utility (see Figure 19-3).

4. Follow the on-screen instructions to complete the setup.

5. If the hard drive needs to be formatted, open the network drive's management utility.

    The manufacturer's documentation should provide instructions on how to access the management utility. You may see a desktop icon or a link in the Windows Start menu, or you may need to access the drive by entering its IP address in your Web browser.

6. Click the link to open the administration controls (see Figure 19-4).

7. Click HD Format and follow the on-screen instructions to format the hard drive. Any data currently on the drive will be lost.

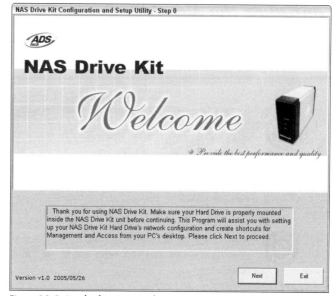

Figure 19-3: Run the drive's setup utility.

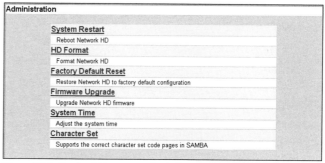

Figure 19-4: Your hard drive may need to be formatted.

Configure the Network Drive

1. Open the drive's management screen.

2. Change the default password to a password of your own creation.

    Changing the password will help protect your data from access by Internet-based intruders.

3. Open the Host Name controls and enter a host name, workgroup name, and description for the drive, as shown in Figure 19-5.

    The host name should be descriptive enough that network users will recognize it as the network storage drive. The workgroup name should be the same workgroup name used by your Windows computers.

4. Click the link to open the IP address controls and make sure that DHCP is enabled (see Figure 19-6).

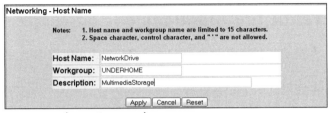

Figure 19-5: The Host Name controls.

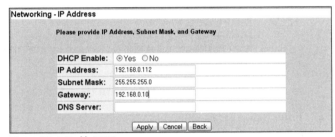

Figure 19-6: Enable DHCP.

 If you enable DHCP, you can leave the IP address and other fields blank, because the DHCP server in your router will automatically assign the drive an IP address.

Create User Accounts

1. Open the network drive's management utility and then open the Share screen.

2. Click the link for User Configuration or User Accounts, depending on your drive.

3. In the User Configuration screen, select the type of account that you want to create and click the Add button (see Figure 19-7).

    A power user has full read and write access to all folders of the drive. The All user type can read and write to the drive's shared folders. A guest user can only read files in shared folders, and is not allowed to change or delete any files.

4. Enter a user name and password for the new user (see Figure 19-8).

5. Decide whether or not the user will be allowed access by way of FTP.

    FTP access should be disabled unless you know that a specific user will be using FTP.

6. Click Apply to create the user account.

    To delete an account, select it in the User Configuration window and click Delete.

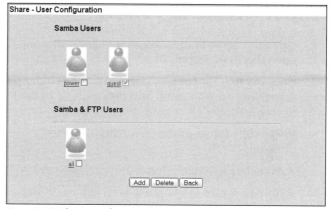

Figure 19-7: The User configuration screen.

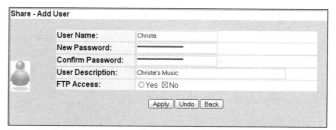

Figure 19-8: Enter a user name and password for the new user.

Control Access to Folders

1. Open the network drive's management utility and then open the Share screen.

2. Click the link for Folder Configuration or Folder Access, depending on your drive, and perform one of the following actions:

   - To add a folder to the drive, click Add (see Figure 19-9).

   - To delete a folder, select it and click Delete.

   - To edit folder access privileges, click the folder's name.

3. In the screen shown in Figure 19-10, set global privileges for all users and control access for individual users.

    The Non-Access setting means the user will not be able to see or access the folder at all. The Read Only setting means users can see and access files in the folder, but not change or delete them.

4. Click Apply to apply your changes.

Figure 19-9: Add a new folder to the drive.

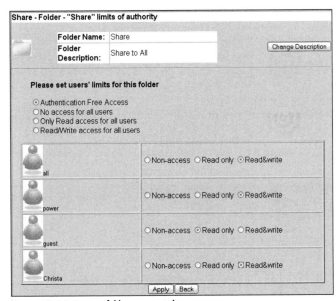

Figure 19-10: Manage folder access privileges.

Access the Network Drive from Windows

1. If the setup utility for the network drive created a desktop icon, double-click it and then proceed to Step 3. Otherwise, choose Start⇨My Network Places.

2. Click View Workgroup Computers under Network Tasks on the left side of the My Network Places window. Double-click the icon for the network drive when it appears.

3. Log in to the drive using an account name and password, as shown in Figure 19-11.

Figure 19-11: Log in to the drive.

 Remember, you must use an account name and password for a valid user account on the network drive, not your local computer. After you are logged in, browse the drive using the Windows Explorer windows just as you would any other drive.

Access the Network Drive from a Mac

1. Open the Finder and then click the Network icon to access network locations.

2. Double-click the network drive's icon.

3. Log in to the drive using an account name and password (see Figure 19-12).

4. Choose a folder which you want to authenticate and click OK. You can now browse the drive using the Finder window.

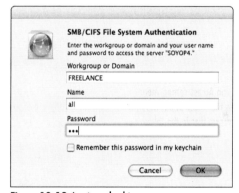

Figure 19-12: Log in to the drive.

 Remember, you must use an account name and password for a valid user account on the network drive, not your local computer.

Project: Connecting to a Digital Media Receiver

The line between personal computers and home entertainment centers has been getting increasingly blurry in recent years, to the point where today that line is essentially gone. In Chapter 18, I discuss how to build a wireless media center based around a computer. But even if you don't want to dedicate a whole computer to home entertainment, you can still connect your home theater to your wireless network using a digital media receiver (DMR).

A DMR is a small device that connects directly to your home theater and offers a connection to your computer network. Most modern DMRs offer Wi-Fi connection, meaning you won't have to string messy Ethernet cables all over your living room. With a DMR you can use your home theater to play media that is stored on your PC in another room. Virtually all DMRs can play music, and most can also be used to watch movies or view photos. This chapter shows how to use a DMR with your home network.

Chapter
20

Get ready to . . .

Configure the Digital Media Receiver

1. Choose a digital media receiver that supports the type of media you want to play.

     Some DMRs only play audio, while others can also show pictures and video. If you are accessing Windows Media files, try to choose a DMR that displays the Windows Media PlaysForSure logo. This logo indicates that the manufacturer has tested the device and certified it to work with Windows Media Player. Likewise, if you have an iTunes library make sure you buy a DMR that displays the iTunes logo. Some DMRs can play both Windows Media and iTunes media.

2. Connect the receiver to an Ethernet port on your router and follow the manufacturer's instructions to configure the DMR's network settings.

3. If the DMR has built-in Wi-Fi, disconnect the Ethernet cable to use the device wirelessly (see Figure 20-1).

Install Windows Media Connect

1. Download the latest version of the Windows Media Connect software from Microsoft.

     Windows Media Connect is required to make connections between Windows Media files on your computer and a DMR. To download Windows Media Connect, visit www.microsoft.com/windows/windowsmedia/devices/wmconnect/.

2. Locate the downloaded installation file and double-click it to begin installation (see Figure 20-2).

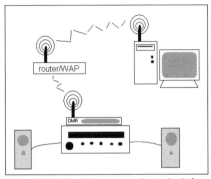

Figure 20-1: The DMR can get media wirelessly from your computer.

Figure 20-2: Begin the Windows Media Connect Installation.

3. Follow the on-screen instructions to complete installation.

4. Choose Start➪All Programs➪Windows Media Connect to launch Windows Media Connect.

5. If you see your digital media receiver listed in the screen shown in Figure 20-3, select it. Otherwise, just click Next.

6. In the screen, choose whether or not you want to share the listed folders (see Figure 20-4). Then you can

   • Click Finish to close the wizard, unless you chose Let Me Choose Which Folders for Folder Sharing, in which case you should click Next.

   • Click Add and browse to the folder or folders you want to share. When you are done selecting folders, click Finish.

 The default choice shares the My Pictures, My Music, and My Video folders in your My Documents folder, as well as the equivalent folders in the Shared Documents folder.

 Only share folders that you use for storing pictures, music, and movie files.

 After you finish running the wizard, you should see a Windows Media Connect icon in the Windows system tray, which is the area in the lower-right corner of the screen next to the clock. Double-click the Windows Media Connect icon to adjust media connect settings.

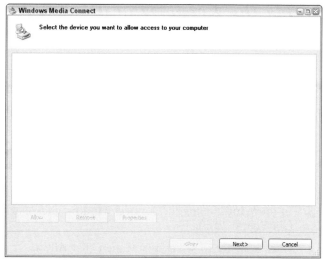

Figure 20-3: If your DMR is listed here, select it before clicking Next.

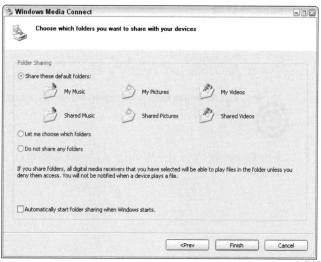

Figure 20-4: Select folders to share.

Enable the Receiver in Windows Media Connect

1. Make sure that your digital media receiver is turned on and connected to your network.

2. Double-click the Windows Media Connect icon in the Windows system tray.

    You can also open Windows Media Connect from the Start menu. Choose Start➪All Programs➪Windows Media Connect to launch the program.

3. In the Windows Media Connect window, click Devices (see Figure 20-5).

4. Click a device to select it, and then click Allow.

5. To block a device from accessing media on your computer, select the device in the list and then click Deny.

6. Click Settings.

7. If you want to automatically allow new devices to connect to your media, select the Automatically Allow New Devices check box (see Figure 20-6).

    Read the warning message that appears and click Yes to accept the change.

8. Click Close to close the Windows Media Connect window.

Figure 20-5: Allow or deny access for media devices.

Figure 20-6: Allow new DMRs to connect to your computer automatically.

Share a Windows Media Folder.

1. Double-click the Windows Media Connect icon in the Windows system tray to open Windows Media Connect.

   You can also open Windows Media Connect from the Start menu. Choose Start➪All Programs➪Windows Media Connect to launch the program.

2. In the Windows Media Connect window, click Settings.

3. If folder sharing has not started, an on-screen message tells you the status of folder sharing click Start.)

4. Click Sharing to open the folder sharing screen (see Figure 20-7).

5. To add a folder, click the Add button.

6. In the Add Sharing Information window, click the Browse button and browse to a folder that you want to share.

7. Give the folder a descriptive name (see Figure 20-8) and then click OK.

8. To stop sharing a specific folder, select it in the list of currently shared folders in the Windows Media Connect window and then click Remove.

9. Click Close to close the Windows Media Connect window.

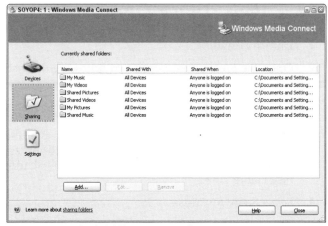

Figure 20-7: Decide which folders you want to share.

Figure 20-8: Browse to additional folders that you want to share.

Share Your iTunes Library

1. Launch iTunes.

2. Open the Preferences window by following these steps:

   - **Mac:** Choose iTunes⇨Preferences.

   - **Windows:** Choose Edit⇨Preferences.

3. On a Mac, click the Sharing button at the top of the preferences dialog box to reveal sharing options, as shown in Figure 20-9. In Windows, click the Sharing tab (see Figure 20-10).

4. Select Share My Music.

5. Choose whether you want to share your entire library, or just certain playlists. If you only want to share some playlists, select Share Selected Playlists and place a check mark next to each playlist that you want to share.

6. Enter a descriptive name for the shared media library in the Shared Name field.

    If you want to password protect your computer, place a check mark next to Require Password and enter a password. Keep in mind, however, that many DMRs will not be able to access password-protected media.

7. Click OK to close iTunes preferences and save your changes.

    Leave iTunes running on your computer. Most DMRs cannot access music shared from an iTunes library if iTunes is not running the host computer.

Figure 20-9: iTunes sharing options.

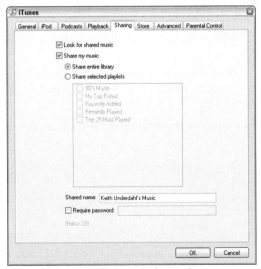

Figure 20-10: The Windows version of iTunes sharing options.

Play Media

1. Turn on your digital media receiver and make sure it is connected to your network.

    When the DMR connects to your network, it should automatically detect media folders that you shared earlier in this chapter.

2. Use the DMR's remote control to select a shared media folder (see Figure 20-11).

3. Use the DMR's menu to browse folders and select media to play.

    If the DMR is unable to locate some of your media, make sure that the missing media is shared properly, and that the computer storing the media is turned on and connected to the network. Also double-check that the media is in a format that is supported by your DMR.

Stream Internet Radio to the Receiver

1. Open your media player program and create a playlist for radio stations. Give the playlist a descriptive name, such as Radio Stations or Internet Radio.

2. Open the Internet radio tuner and click and drag radio stations to your radio playlist. The playlist in Figure 20-12 includes five Internet radio stations.

3. On your DMR, select the radio station playlist and choose a radio station to which you want to listen.

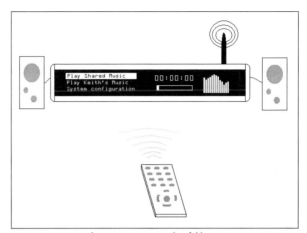

Figure 20-11: Use the DMR's remote to select folders.

Figure 20-12: Create a playlist for Internet radio stations.

Project: Turning Your Pocket PC into a Remote Control

*I*f you've recently purchased a modern Pocket PC equipped with Wi-Fi and Bluetooth, you probably spent a fair sum of money on it, and now you're looking for new things to do with the Pocket PC to justify its purchase price. Meanwhile, in your living room are three or four different remotes, all designed to control different pieces of gear, with none of them able to control your wireless media server computer.

You are in luck, because media remote programs can turn your Pocket PC into a powerful and versatile remote control. Some programs — like Rudeo Play & Control (www.rudeo.com) — allow you to control the media player software on your media server computer from anywhere in range of your Wi-Fi network. This chapter shows you how to install and use remote control software on your Pocket PC.

 Chapter 15 covers setting up and using wireless network connections on a Pocket PC.

Install Remote Control Software

1. Install Windows Media Connect on your media server computer. (For just the steps on how to do so, refer to Chapter 20.)

2. Install the latest version of Windows Media Player both on your media server and your Pocket PC.

    Most remote control programs require Windows Media Player 9 or better; check the software producer's documentation for specific requirements. You can download Windows Media Player for free from www.microsoft.com/windows/windowsmedia/.

3. Connect your Pocket PC to your computer using a sync cable and ActiveSync. (Make sure that the Pocket PC is powered-on.)

4. Launch the installer for the remote control program.

5. Review any special instructions in the installer. In Figure 21-1, for example, the Rudeo Play & Control program requires .NET Framework software to be installed on both the desktop PC and Pocket PC.

6. When you see the message shown in Figure 21-2, check the screen of the Pocket PC for special installation steps. In most cases, you will have to confirm installation and choose an installation location.

    If possible, install the remote software on the Pocket PC's internal memory, and not on removable storage media such as an SD card.

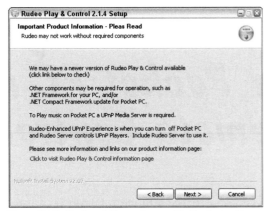

Figure 21-1: Heed special instructions provided by the installer.

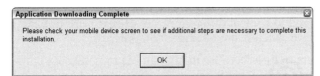

Figure 21-2: Check the Pocket PC for additional installation steps.

Connect the Remote to the Media Server

1. Make sure that Windows Media Connect is running on your server PC and folder sharing is enabled.

     Chapter 20 covers Windows Media Connect.

2. Launch the remote software on your Pocket PC.

3. Tap the Menu icon and choose Setup (see Figure 21-3).

4. In the Setup screen, select the desired media server, as shown in Figure 21-4.

5. Tap OK to close Settings and return to the main screen.

     If you have difficulty making a connection between your Pocket PC, you may need to adjust firewall settings on the server PC to allow the remote software to access the network.

Figure 21-3: Open the remote program's setup screen.

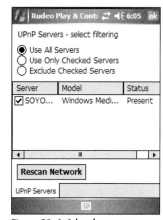

Figure 21-4: Select the server you want to control.

Build the Media Library

1. In the remote control program on your Pocket PC, tap the device menu (see Figure 21-5) and then choose the device you want to control.

2. Read the warning message that appears, and then tap OK to download the library to your Pocket PC.

 Don't worry, the actual media files will remain on the server computer. When the remote software downloads the library, it simply downloads a list of the items that are in your library.

3. After the library is downloaded, tap the Music Note icon along the top of the remote control program to view your music library (see Figure 21-6).

4. Tap the Film Strip icon to view your list of available videos.

5. Tap the Radio icon to browse available Internet radio stations.

6. Tap the Playlist icon to access playlists that you have created in Windows Media Player.

Figure 21-5: Choose the device you want to control.

Figure 21-6: View your library.

Play Media

1. Locate some media that you want to play in the media library (see Figure 21-7).

2. Tap to place a check mark next to songs that you want to hear, and then tap the green arrow at the bottom of the screen to queue the media up for play.

3. Tap the Play Control icon on the far left side of the upper toolbar to open the player controls (see Figure 21-8).

    Although the server computer must have Windows Media Connect running, it is not necessary to launch Windows Media Player on the server computer. When Windows Media Connect is running, the media plays automatically.

4. Use the playback controls to control playback.

    The controls include standard playback controls such as Play, Pause, Stop, Next Track, Previous Track, and a volume slider.

5. Tap a song in the current playlist and then use the arrow buttons at the bottom of the screen to move the song up or down in the playback order.

    Songs at the top of the list play first.

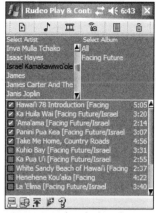

Figure 21-7: Place check marks next to songs you want to hear.

Figure 21-8: Use these buttons to control playback.

Project: Adding a Wireless Print Server to Your Network

*O*ne of the main purposes for creating a home network is so that you can share stuff between your various computers. This *stuff* can include files, your Internet connection, and of course, printers. When everything is properly configured, any computer should be able to use a shared network printer.

The traditional way to share a printer with a network is to first connect the printer to one computer, and then set up printer sharing on that computer so that other PCs could share the printer. But doing this is inconvenient because it means that the computer connected to the printer has to be turned on and connected to the network before anyone else can print. Now, thanks to Wi-Fi, you can share a printer wirelessly using a wireless print server, a device designed specifically to connect printers to Wi-Fi networks. When you connect your printer to a wireless print server, any computer on your network can access the printer directly through the network. In this chapter, you find out how to set up and use a wireless print server.

Select a Wireless Print Server

1. Make sure the print server is a wireless print server.

2. Determine to which type of port your printer connects:

   • Centronics parallel port (see Figure 22-1).

   • DB-25 parallel port (see Figure 22-2).

   • USB port (see Figure 22-3).

 Most modern printers connect directly to a USB port, so a print server with USB port is a safe bet in most cases. If the print server has a Centronics parallel connector, it's probably designed to plug directly into the Centronics connector on the printer.

3. Purchase a print server with enough ports to accommodate all of your printers.

 If you only have one printer then you probably just need a single-port print server. But if you have multiple printers, purchase a multi-port print server with enough ports of the correct type for all of your printers.

4. Check the security features supported by the print server.

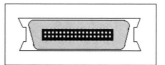

Figure 22-1: A Centronics parallel port.

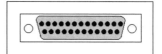

Figure 22-2: The DB-25 parallel connector.

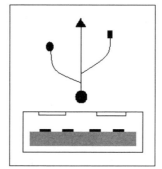

Figure 22-3: A USB port.

 Many print servers support only WEP encryption and not WPA. If you use WPA encryption on your network, a WEP-only print server will not be compatible.

Set Up the Hardware

1. For the initial configuration, connect the print server to your router/WAP using an Ethernet cable (see Figure 22-4).

2. Make sure that the printer's power is turned off and then connect the printer to the print server.

3. Turn on the printer and then connect the power cord for the print server.

4. Configure the print server's Wi-Fi connection (see the following task).

5. After you have configured the print server's Wi-Fi connection, disconnect the Ethernet cable so that the print server connects to your network wirelessly (see Figure 22-5).

 If the print server becomes unable to connect to the wireless network after you disconnect the Ethernet cable, disconnect the print server's power cable for several seconds and then reconnect it. If the problem persists, try rebooting the router/WAP as well.

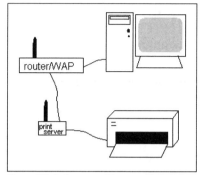

Figure 22-4: Connect an Ethernet cable between the print server and router.

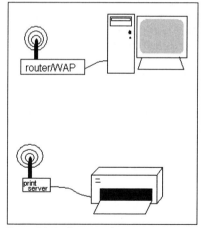

Figure 22-5: After setup, the print server can communicate wirelessly.

Configure the Print Server

1. Install the print server utility program on one of your network computers.

2. On the computer on which you installed the utility program, choose Start➪Run.

3. In the Run dialog box, type CMD and click OK.

4. At the command prompt, type **ipconfig**, as shown in Figure 22-6, and press Enter.

5. Make a note of the IP address, subnet mask, and default gateway that appear (see Figure 22-6).

 The subnet mask and default gateway are the same for each computer on your network. Each computer also shares the first three segments of the IP address, but the last segment of the IP address is unique to each computer and wireless device.

6. Type **EXIT** and press Enter to close the command prompt window.

7. Run the configuration utility for the print server, as shown in Figure 22-7.

 After the print server utility software is installed, you should be able to run it from the Start menu.

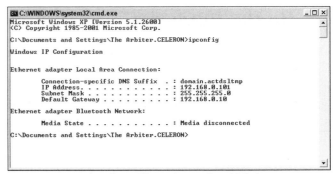

Figure 22-6: Write down the IP address, subnet mask, and default gateway.

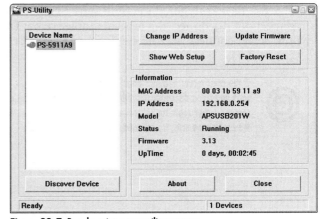

Figure 22-7: Run the print server utility program.

8. Click Change IP address.

> In some print server utility programs, the IP address settings may be located in a menu.

9. Select the DHCP Automatically Assign option and click OK.

> In most cases, having an IP address automatically assigned to the print server is preferable. However, if the print server does not work with automatic IP assignment, follow the next few steps to set the network addresses manually. Otherwise, skip ahead to Step 12.

10. Enter the first three segments of your network's IP address (see Figure 22-8). For the last segment of the IP address, enter a number between zero and 254.

11. Enter your network's subnet mask and default gateway and click OK to save your changes.

12. Open the print server's Web browser configuration utility. Locate the Wireless settings and enter your SSID, WEP keys, and other Wi-Fi security settings (see Figure 22-9).

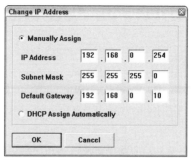

Figure 22-8: Enter network address information here.

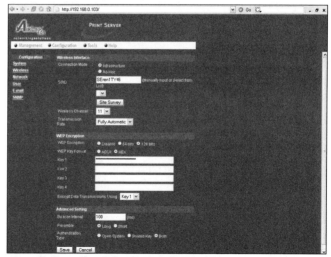

Figure 22-9: Enter Wi-Fi security settings into the print server.

Install Printer Drivers on Network Computers

1. Insert the setup disc that came with your printer in the computer from which you want to print.

2. Use the installation utility to install the printer drivers (see Figure 22-10).

3. Repeat the installation on each network computer from which you plan to print documents.

 In some cases it may not be necessary to install printer drivers. Printer drivers for many modern printers are built-in to Windows XP and Mac OS X.

Print from Windows

1. Open the Windows Control Panel and then double-click the Printers and Faxes icon.

2. Click Add a Printer under Printer Tasks on the left side of the screen.

3. Click Next in the first screen of the Add Printer Wizard and then choose Network Printer in the second screen.

4. Choose to Browse for a printer and then browse to your print server, as shown in Figure 22-11.

5. When you are prompted to do so, select the printer driver for the network printer. You can now print to the network printer from any application. Simply select the network printer in the printer selection menu of each program's respective Print dialog box.

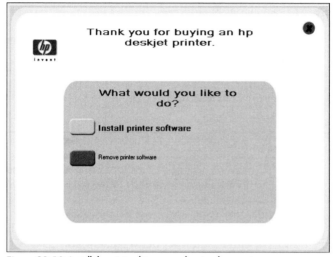

Figure 22-10: Install the printer driver on each network computer.

Figure 22-11: Browse to the print server.

Print from Mac OS X

1. Choose Apple⇨System Preferences and then click the Print & Fax icon in the System Preferences window.

2. Click the Plus (+) sign in the Print & Fax window.

3. In the Printer Browser, shown in Figure 22-12, click Default Browser and then click the name of your printer using the AppleTalk connection type.

 The Printer Name listed in the Printer Browser may actually be the name of the print server instead of the printer.

4. Choose your printer's brand in the Print Using menu.

5. Choose your printer's model from the model menu that appears (see Figure 22-12).

6. Click Add. You can now print to the network printer from any application. Simply select the network printer in the printer selection menu of each program's respective Print dialog box.

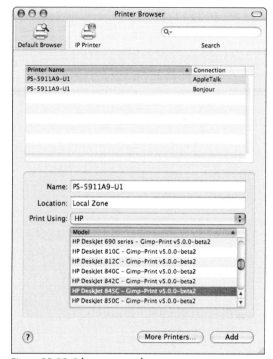

Figure 22-12: Select your network printer.

Project: Setting Up Your Own Hotspot

*W*hen you set up a wireless home network, you normally spend a lot of time making sure that your network is private. But what if you want friends and family to be able to use your wireless network when they visit? Or what if you have a small business and want to give your customers Internet access when they're at your store?

The solution is to create your own hotspot. With a hotspot, your friends or customers can easily access the Internet while they're at your home or business. If you have a small business such as a coffee shop, motel, or restaurant, Wi-Fi access may be particularly appealing to your customers and may help improve your sales. This chapter shows you how to set up a public or semi-public hotspot of your own.

 Do not connect your business computers to your hotspot. People who use your hotspot could possibly access other computers that are connected to the hotspot, and if your business computers are connected your sensitive data could be compromised. Set up a separate network to use for your business PCs.

Choose an Access Point

1. Select a wireless access point (WAP) that supports as many 802.11 Wi-Fi formats as possible.

    At a bare minimum, the WAP you choose should support 802.11b because that is the most widely used format. Some WAPs also support 802.11a and 802.11g.

2. Make sure that the WAP also has a built-in router, like the one shown in Figure 23-1.

    Your wireless access point needs to have a built-in router so that DHCP can automatically assign IP addresses to each computer that joins the network. The router/WAP in Figure 23-1 was supplied by my DSL service provider and even has a built-in DSL modem. This unit would make setting up a hotspot very easy.

3. Choose an access point designed for outdoor use if you want to extend your hotspot into harsher environments.

4. Ensure that the access point conforms to local fire codes.

5. Consider a WAP with built-in access control, if this is a feature you need.

6. Make sure the WAP can accept external, high-gain antennas. Most WAPs use a standard coaxial antenna connector.

Figure 23-1: This WAP is also a router and a DSL modem.

 Most municipalities have special fire safety codes for businesses, and some of the cheap mass-market WAPs offered to home users don't meet local fire safety codes. Check your local codes and the documentation for your WAP to ensure that it complies.

 Access control allows you to limit hotspot users to your customers. With access control, customers must enter a user name and password to use the hotspot.

Deal with Your Internet Service Provider

1. Review your Internet Service Provider's (ISP) terms of service agreement carefully for any limitations that might prevent you from running a Wi-Fi hotspot.

2. Contact the ISP and tell them that you want to create a hotspot.

3. If possible, upgrade the speed of your Internet connection. A 256k DSL connection may be fine for only a few computers, as shown in Figure 23-2, but if you have many users, as shown in Figure 23-3, the connection will be too slow to handle all of the traffic.

4. Find out if your ISP or another company offers hotspot services that can be used in your business.

 If you think you'll have a lot of hotspot users and you are concerned about managing it properly or dealing with unforeseen costs, consider contracting the hotspot service out to your ISP or another service provider. Keep in mind that generally speaking, the less hotspot access costs your customers, the more it will cost you.

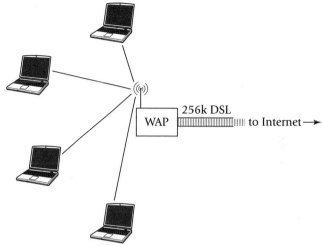

Figure 23-2: A 256k DSL connection can support a few computers using e-mail and the Internet.

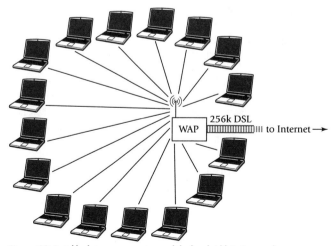

Figure 23-3: Add a lot more computers and the bandwidth isn't enough.

Configure the Access Point

1. Make sure that the hotspot's WAP is not part of your personal network.

    Some business-oriented WAPs support multiple SSIDs, allowing you to manage both public and private networks using the same WAP.

2. Use a Web browser to log in to the WAP's control panel.

3. Change the WAP's administrator password so that it is no longer the factory default. Use a strong password that includes a combination of letters and numbers.

4. Locate the wireless network controls (see Figure 23-4).

5. Set an SSID that is recognizable and easy to type.

    Choose an SSID that identifies your business or location. Remind your users that the SSID is case sensitive.

6. Determine whether or not you want to broadcast the SSID and adjust broadcast settings.

    If you don't broadcast the SSID, you can more easily control who gets on the network. However, this also makes it a lot harder for users to log-on. If the SSID is not broadcast, users will have to manually enter the SSID to join your network; it will not show up automatically in their network lists.

7. Disable proprietary speed boosting technologies, if your WAP incorporates them.

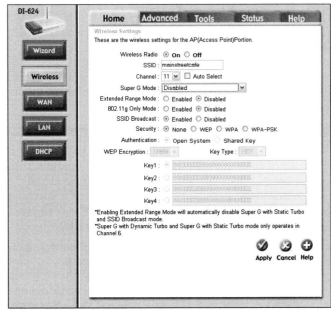

Figure 23-4: Broadcast the SSID.

 Most companies offer proprietary technologies that allow theoretical networking speeds faster than 54Mbps, which is the speed of 802.11g. Most of your users will probably have different brands of equipment, meaning they can't take advantage of the speed boosting technologies. In some rare cases the speed boosting features can cause compatibility issues with other brands of equipment. Furthermore, you probably don't want to encourage the high-bandwidth usage that can result from speed-boosting technologies.

8. Determine whether you need to use WEP or WPA encryption and adjust settings accordingly.

 Generally speaking, you do not want to use encryption on your hotspot. For more on configuring and using encryption, see Chapter 6.

9. Set the transmission (Tx) rate to 11 Mbps if you are concerned about bandwidth, as shown in Figure 23-5.

 Using 11Mbps ensures compatibility with 802.11a/b/g devices, and it should be plenty of speed for e-mail and Web browsing. By slowing the Wi-Fi network speed down to 11Mbps, you discourage high-bandwidth usage such as file downloading. Usually the Tx Rate can be controlled on the Wireless screen of your WAP's control panel, or as in the case in Figure 23-5 on the Performance screen.

10. Locate the DHCP server controls (see Figure 23-6) and make sure that the DHCP server is enabled.

11. Set an IP address range that is adequate for the number of computers you plan to use the network.

 The numbers in IP addresses can range between 0 and 255. In Figure 23-6, the range is 100–199, meaning that 100 computers can use the network simultaneously. If you want to limit it to a lower number, reduce the allowable range of IP addresses.

12. Change the IP address Lease Time to a shorter time period, such as one hour.

13. Save your settings and close the WAP control panel.

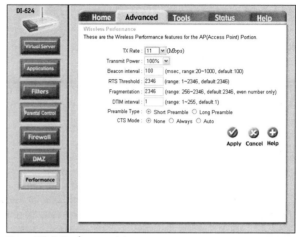

Figure 23-5: Set the transmission rate.

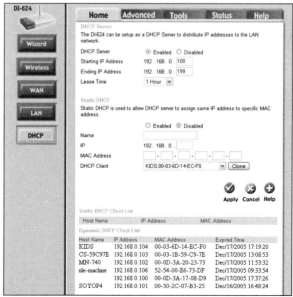

Figure 23-6: Adjust DHCP settings for your hotspot.

Control Access to the Hotspot

1. Remind your customers about good security practices.

Customers should disable file sharing on their computers when using the hotspot, and turn off their computers or disable the Wi-Fi adapter when they are done using the network.

2. Log in to your WAP's control panel.

3. Review the traffic statistics for your hotspot (see Figure 23-7).

You should review traffic statistics at least daily. Excessive wireless traffic may indicate that your hotspot users are using the connection to download large files. To discourage this use, reduce the transmission speed of your WAP as described earlier in this chapter, or implement more stringent access controls.

4. During business hours, regularly check the number of wireless clients currently connected to your hotspot (see Figure 23-8).

In Figure 23-8, three computers are connected to the network. If I look around and see that only one person in my store is using a computer, then it is likely that people outside the business are stealing access.

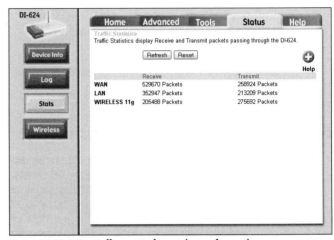

Figure 23-7: Review traffic statistics for your hotspot frequently.

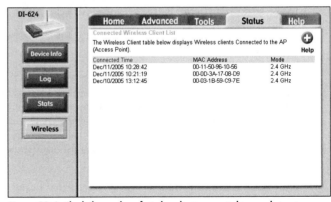

Figure 23-8: Check the number of wireless clients connected to your hotspot.

5. If your hotspot is only for the use of friends and family, disable SSID broadcast and set up basic encryption, as I describe in Chapter 6.

6. If tighter access control is required, install and use a hotspot access control program, as shown in Figure 23-9, or a dedicated hotspot appliance that serves as a WAP and log-in controller.

 The access control program or appliance should present your users with a simple Web browser-based log-in screen, such as the one shown in Figure 23-9. Hotspot access programs include ControlAP (www. controlap.com) and PatronSoft FirstSpot (www. patronsoft.com). Hotspot appliances include the Boingo Hot Spot in a Box (www.boingo.com), Gemtek P-560 (www.gemtek-systems.com) or Netopia Hotspot Starter Kit (www.netopia.com).

Deactivate the Hotspot

1. Log in to your WAP's control panel.

2. Locate the wireless radio controls (see Figure 23-10).

3. Turn off the wireless radio.

4. Save your settings and close the WAP control panel.

 You should deactivate your hotspot whenever you are closed for business or do not otherwise want users accessing the hotspot.

Figure 23-9: Use software that utilizes a browser-based log-in screen.

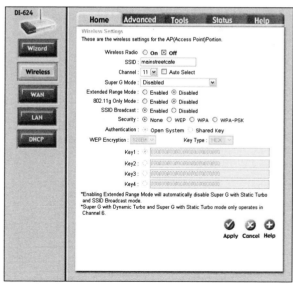

Figure 23-10: Turn off the wireless radio to deactivate the hotspot.

Project: Voice Chatting with Your Wireless Network

*T*ext chatting is almost as old as the Internet itself. A more recent development, however, is the growing popularity of voice chat over the Internet. If you have a broadband Internet connection, you can save long distance phone charges by making your calls online. And if you have a wireless computer, you can use it to make your Internet calls from anywhere in your home.

Several free programs are available that let you make Internet calls. You find out about two of the most popular programs — Skype (www.skype.com) and Google Talk (www.google.com/talk/) — in this chapter. In addition to an Internet voice chat program, you also need speakers and a microphone. At the end of this chapter, I show you how to use either Skype or Google Talk with a wireless Bluetooth headset.

 Chapter 14 provides information on configuring Bluetooth headsets and other Bluetooth gear for use with your computer.

Install Skype

1. Visit www.skype.com and click the Download link. Follow the links to download a version of Skype appropriate for your computer.

 Note any special installation instructions on the Web site. As of this writing, versions of Skype are available for Linux, Mac OS X, Pocket PC, and Windows.

2. When the installation file is downloaded, locate it on your computer. Double-click the file to begin installation.

3. Follow the instructions on-screen to install Skype. When you get to the last screen of the installation program, select the Launch Skype check box and click Finish.

4. In the Create Account window that appears the first time you launch Skype, shown in Figure 24-1, enter a Skype name and password.

5. Click Next, fill in the optional information if desired, and click Next again.

 If the Skype name you entered is already being used by someone else, Skype will automatically recommend some alternatives. You can also try entering a different name if you wish. The first time you log into Skype a tour will introduce the key features of the program.

6. If you already have a Skype account and are simply installing Skype on a new computer, click the Existing Users tab in the account creation dialog box (see Figure 24-2). Enter your account name and password to log in.

 You can create multiple Skype accounts on the same computer. Simply choose File⇨Log Off, and then choose File⇨Log in as a New User to create a new account.

Figure 24-1: The Create Account window.

Figure 24-2: Log in to an account.

Find Skype Users

1. Open Skype.

   If you are not automatically logged in when you launch Skype, choose File⇨Log In as a New User to log in.

2. On the Skype toolbar, click Add Contact.

3. Enter a name, Skype name, or e-mail address and click Search.

   If your search yields too many results, close the Add a Contact window and click Search in the main Skype window. Doing this opens a search screen that allows you to tailor your search by location, gender, and other criteria.

4. In the list of results (see Figure 24-3), select the name of the person you want to add to your list of Skype contacts and click Add Selected Contact.

5. In the authorization request window that appears (see Figure 24-4), choose whether or not you want the person to be able to see when you are online.

   A default text message appears, but you can customize the message if you wish. Simply delete the existing text and type a new message.

6. Click OK. After the contact has authorized you, his or her name appears in your list of contacts in the main Skype window.

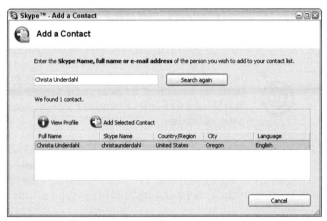

Figure 24-3: Add someone to your list of contacts.

Figure 24-4: Contacts must authorize calls from you.

Make a Call with Skype

1. Click a name in your contacts list (see Figure 24-5).

   You can only place live calls to people who are currently online and not involved in another call. If a person is online the button next to his or her name will be green. If the person is offline, you can send a voice-mail message.

2. Click the Call button at the bottom of the Skype window. Skype attempts the call and a ringing phone sounds in your computer speakers. The ring tone also sounds in the other person's speakers and a notification message appears.

3. Click the phone button (vertical receiver) in the call notification window to answer an incoming call (see Figure 24-6).

4. During the call, choose Call⇨Mute Microphone to temporarily mute your outgoing audio.

5. Cick the End Call button (horizontal receiver) to end a call. Either participant can end a call.

   You can also conduct conference calls using Skype. To do so, click Conference on the Skype toolbar, and then select conference participants from your contacts list. Conference calls can have up to five people (including the host) although you may find that audio quality diminishes exponentially with each additional conference participant.

Figure 24-5: Select someone in your contacts list.

Figure 24-6: Answer or end the call.

Call POTS Phone Numbers with Skype

1. To place calls from Skype to land lines or mobile phones using POTS (Plain Old Telephone System) phone numbers, visit www.skype.com and click the SkypeOut link.

2. Follow the instructions to purchase Skype Credit online.

3. In Skype, click the Dial tab.

4. Enter the country code and phone number to place a call (see Figure 24-7).

5. Conduct the call (see Figure 24-8). Click the End Call button to terminate the call when you're done.

 Skype cannot be used to call emergency numbers, such as 911. If you have an emergency, make sure you use a land line or cell phone to place the call.

6. To get a phone number that other people can use to call you from any land line or mobile phone, visit www.skype.com and click the SkypeIn link.

7. Follow the instructions on the Web site to subscribe to a SkypeIn number. Skype automatically provides you with a phone number that others can use to call you from almost any telephone. Callers incur long distance phone charges in accordance with the policies of their long distance carrier.

 When you select a country and locale for your SkypeIn number, choose a number that is close to the majority of people who will be calling you. For example, if people in California call your United Kingdom-based SkypeIn number, they will pay international call rates to their long distance provider, even if you actually take the calls using Skype in New York.

Figure 24-7: Call almost any phone number with SkypeOut.

Figure 24-8: Conduct the call.

Install Google Talk

1. Visit www.google.com/talk/ and click the Download Google Talk button.

 Google Talk requires a Gmail account. If you don't have a Gmail account, click the Get An Account link on the Google Talk page and follow the instructions to create a Gmail account. Gmail accounts are free but typically require that you provide some information such as a mobile phone number.

2. When the Google Talk installation file is downloaded, locate the file and then double-click it to begin installation.

3. Follow the instructions on-screen to complete the simple installation process.

4. After installation, enter your Gmail username and password in the login screen, shown in Figure 24-9.

5. After you are logged in to Google Talk, click the Settings link near the top of the Google Talk window.

6. In the Settings window, review the General settings (see Figure 24-10).

7. If you don't want Google Talk to automatically launch every time you start Windows, deselect Start Automatically When Starting Windows check box.

8. Review other settings and click OK when you are done.

Figure 24-9: Log in to Google Talk.

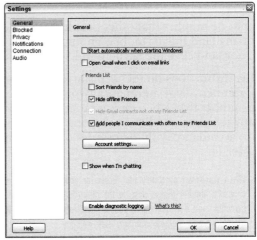

Figure 24-10: Adjust Google Talk settings.

Find Google Talk Users

1. Launch Google Talk if it is not already open.

2. Click Add Friend in the lower-right corner of the Google Talk window.

3. In the resulting Invitation screen (see Figure 24-11), enter the e-mail address of the person you want to add to your contacts list and Click Next.

 You can enter any e-mail address, whether the person has a Gmail account or not.

• If the person already has a Gmail account, you will see a screen congratulating you for successfully adding the contact.

• If the person does not have a Gmail account, you see the screen shown in Figure 24-12. Edit the invitation text if desired and click Next.

 Pay attention to the number of free Gmail invites remaining on your account. Gmail allows you a fixed number of invites, so use them carefully. The screen with the invitation text (Figure 24-12) also lists your remaining Gmail invites.

Figure 24-11: Enter the e-mail address of contacts you want to add.

Figure 24-12: Gmail invites non-Gmail users to join.

Talk with Google Talk

1. To place a voice call with Google Talk, locate the person you want to call in your contacts list, as shown in Figure 24-13.

2. If the person is online and available — a green dot means the person is available — click the phone icon next to the name. The phone begins to ring.

3. When the person answers the call, begin talking.

4. To text chat with someone, double-click his or her name in your contacts list.

5. Type text and press Enter on your keyboard to send the text (see Figure 24-14).

6. Click the End Call button to terminate the call.

 Text chat is especially handy for sending Web URLs during voice calls. When you sent a URL through text chat, the other person can simply click on the URL like a hyperlink to open it in a Web browser.

 If you have an important message to send to someone who is offline, double-click the person's name in your contacts list and send a text chat message. The text message will be automatically sent the next time the user goes online.

Figure 24-13: Green dots indicate available contacts.

Figure 24-14: Google Talk also supports text chat.

Chat with a Bluetooth Headset

1. Make sure your computer is set up to utilize wireless Bluetooth headsets. Turn on the Bluetooth headset and create a partnership between the headset and your computer. See Chapter 14 for details.

2. Open Skype and choose Tools⇨Options to configure Skype to use a Bluetooth headset.

3. On the left side of the resulting Options window, click Sound Devices, as shown in Figure 24-15.

4. Choose Bluetooth Audio in the Audio In and Audio Out menus.

5. Choose Windows Default Device in the Ringing menu, and select the Ring PC Speaker option. Doing so allows you to hear ring tones even if you're not wearing your headset.

6. Click Save to close the Options window.

7. In Google Talk, click the Settings link near the top of the Google Talk window and then click Audio on the left side of the Settings window, as shown in Figure 24-16.

8. Choose Bluetooth Audio in the Input and Output Calls menus.

9. Choose All Devices in the Notifications menu to ensure that you hear ringtones even if you're not wearing the headset.

10. Click OK to close the Settings dialog box.

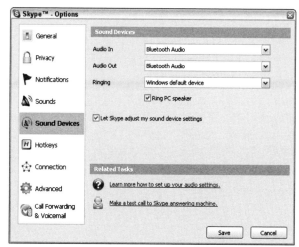

Figure 24-15: Configure Skype to use your Bluetooth headset.

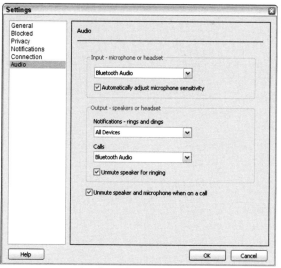

Figure 24-16: Google Talk can also use Bluetooth headsets.

Project: Adding a Wireless Camera to Your Network

Security cameras are nothing new. Business and home owners have been setting up security cameras for many years, but the gear was expensive and required a complex maze of wires to be run through attics or inside walls.

Now, thanks to a new breed of affordable and easy-to-use Wi-Fi-equipped cameras, setting up a home security camera is easy. You can position a Wi-Fi camera anywhere within range of your Wi-Fi network. You can then monitor the camera and record video from it using any computer on your network. You can even set up a special computer just for recording security video if you want. The computer can be an older unit that you don't use much anymore, so long as it has a lot of free hard drive space. In this chapter, you find out how to select and use a wireless camera with your Wi-Fi network.

The exact steps you follow when setting up your security camera may be different from the steps listed here, depending on the brand of camera you buy. However, the general concepts should be the same.

Choose a Wireless Camera

1. Choose a camera that is compatible with 802.11b or 802.11g Wi-Fi networks, such as the one shown in Figure 25-1.

 Many security cameras are marketed as *wireless* security cameras, however they utilize a proprietary radio for wireless transmission rather than 802.11 Wi-Fi. If the camera doesn't specifically say that it is compatible with Wi-Fi networks, it may not work with your network.

2. Determine whether you need a weatherproof camera.

 The camera shown in Figure 25-1 is not weatherproof, but some models are. Weatherproof cameras tend to be more expensive, but they allow you to safely monitor outdoor areas. Also, be aware that if the camera was designed for indoor use, its sensor can be damaged by direct exposure to sunlight.

Install the Camera

1. Connect an Ethernet cable between the camera and your router or a computer.

 A temporary Ethernet connection is usually required during setup. You can reconfigure the camera to work wirelessly later.

2. Connect the camera's power cable and power on the camera.

3. Install the camera's software (see Figure 25-2).

Figure 25-1: This camera has a built-in 802.11g Wi-Fi radio. *Photo courtesy AirLink101.*

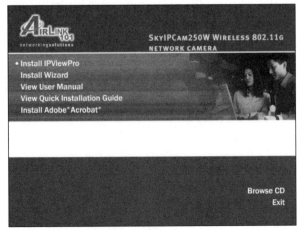

Figure 25-2: Install the camera's software.

4. Write down the following pieces of information for your network:

- The router IP address, subnet mask, and default gateway

- SSID

- Encryption format and keys

5. Configure the camera's software for your network (see Figure 25-3).

 The camera's instructions should describe how to log in to the camera and change network settings. You need to provide the camera with the same SSID and encryption keys used by the rest of your network.

6. When configuration is complete, disconnect the Ethernet cable and test the camera to make sure that it works wirelessly.

7. Move the camera to its permanent position, mount it, and test the wireless connection again (see Figure 25-4).

 In Figure 25-4, I have positioned the camera so that it is looking through a window in my garage. If the camera gets poor or no Wi-Fi reception, move it to a different position. If you need more Wi-Fi range, consider adding a Wi-Fi repeater to your network (refer to Chapter 10).

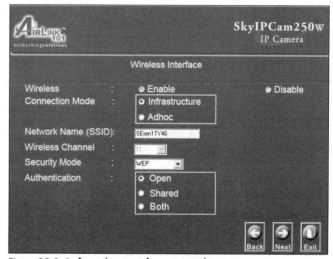

Figure 25-3: Configure the camera for your network.

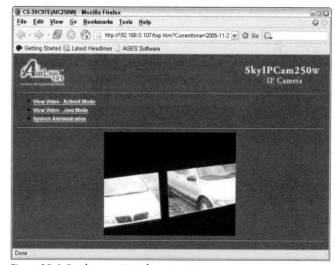

Figure 25-4: Test the camera's wireless connection.

Set Up a Computer to Record Video

1. Install the camera recording software on a computer with lots of free hard drive space.

 Web and security cams typically record at a resolution of 320x240 pixels. At this resolution, you can expect to need about 200–220 MB for every hour of recorded video, or 5–6 GB per day. Higher resolution cameras use exponentially more storage space. Lower resolutions use less space, but also provide vastly inferior video quality.

2. Disable power-saving settings on the recording computer.

 If the computer's hard drive or processor automatically shuts down after a period of computer inactivity, it won't be able to record video from the wireless camera.

3. Launch the camera's recording software and open the configuration window (see Figure 25-5).

4. Location the motion detection controls and activate them if desired.

5. Adjust motion sensitivity.

 Motion sensitivity is usually adjusted with a slider control. You may need to fine-tune this setting later based on what is and isn't recorded by the camera.

6. If possible, create detection regions (see Figure 25-6).

 In Figure 25-6, I have created motion detection regions around the windows, because that is the only area where I want motion detected for recording purposes.

7. Choose notification options for motion detection.

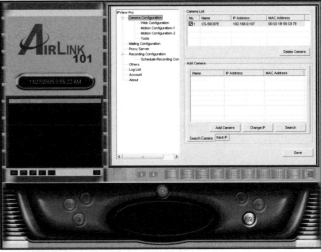

Figure 25-5: Configure the camera's recording software.

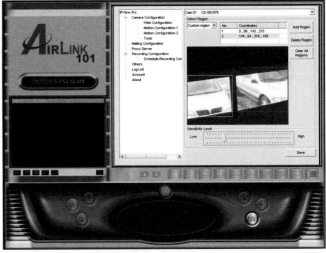

Figure 25-6: Set up motion detection on the camera.

8. Open the recording configuration screen (see Figure 25-7).

9. Set the amount of disk space you want reserved for the Windows operating system (OS).

 I recommend that you reserve at least 1000 MB of free space for Windows. In practice it is a good idea to leave at least 30–40 percent of your hard drive open at any given time. This vastly improves the performance of Windows and your computer.

10. Set the maximum file size for each recorded video file.

11. Choose a storage location for the video files.

12. Choose whether or not you want to recycle storage space.

 When you enable recycling, the recording program overwrites old files when the reserved limit is reached.

13. If you want to record video at a scheduled time every day, open the scheduling page and create a recording schedule.

14. Save your configuration changes and close the configuration screen.

15. Click the Record button and activate recording (see Figure 25-8).

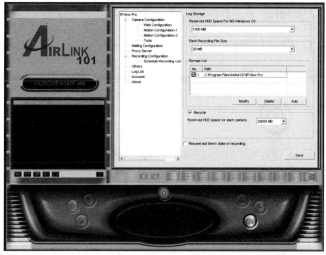

Figure 25-7: Decide how much storage space you want to devote to recorded video.

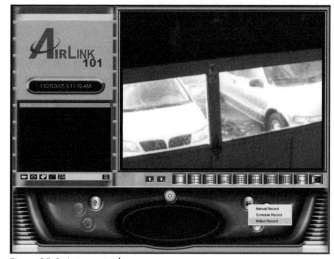

Figure 25-8: Activate recording.

Replay Recorded Video

1. Open the camera's recording utility.

2. Open the playback control panel.

   In the AirLink 101 software, simply click the Play button.

3. Open the folder containing files from your camera (see Figure 25-9).

4. Select the file you want to play and click OK.

   Recorded video files are typically named using the date and time of the recording. In Figure 25-9, I am opening a file named 20051127092319.avi. This file was recorded at 9:23 am on November 27, 2005.

5. Play the file in your media player (see Figure 25-10).

   You can also view files by using Windows Explorer or My Computer to browse to the folder containing the saved video files. There you can double-click on files to view them. You can also copy files from this folder to a safe location in case you need a file for future reference.

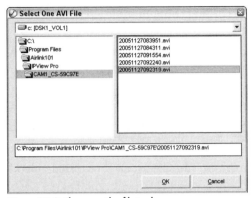

Figure 25-9: Choose a video file to play.

Figure 25-10: View your video files in a media player.

Index

N

X